Praise for *The Bardic Book of Becc*

"*The Bardic Book of Becoming* is a book modern Druids have needed for a long time. Deeply visionary, it offers a look into the spirituality of modern Druidic practice and the underlying beliefs and ideas that sustain it. I would recommend this not only to Druids everywhere but also to all those wishing to know more of this growing spiritual practice."

—John Matthews, author of *The Druid Source Book* and *The Celtic Shaman*

"This book is a paean of love for the Earth from a great smiling bear of a man. Such was Ivan McBeth. There are as many types of Druidism as there are Druids in this world, and in this book Ivan outlines what I call 'Druidry of the Spirit,' the path of the Heart from an English Druid's perspective. Anyone who wants to learn about modern Druids will benefit from this volume, as will those following the path of Nature Spirituality. After reading the book, they will never look at the Sacred Land the same way again."

—Ellen Evert Hopman, Archdruid of Tribe of the Oak and author of *A Legacy of Druids: Conversations with Druid Leaders from Britain, the USA and Canada, Past and Present; Tree Medicine Tree Magic;* and other books

"Ivan McBeth has always meant three things to me: good friend, thoughtful wisdom, and world's foremost stone-circle builder. Bigger than life, he needed two chapters in my book *Stone Circles: A Modern Builder's Guide.* He wouldn't fit in one. But it's the *thoughtful wisdom,* a lifetime's worth, that Ivan's posthumous book is all about. If you want to take up Druidry or are curious about how it would grace your life—and that of Gaia, our planet—this book is the place to start."

—Rob Roy, director of Earthwood Building School and author of seventeen books, including *Cordwood Building*

"*The Bardic Book of Becoming* bubbles with vibrancy and creativity, as did its author. A book of Druid basics, it glints with deeper wisdom. I don't agree with every word but wholly concur with its shimmering intention, its cry for personal responsibility and inspiration."

—Emma Restall Orr, author of *Living with Honour, The Wakeful World,* and other books on Druidry and animism

"Ivan McBeth was a great teacher, guide, and a good friend. His view of the world was magical, visionary, and Shamanistic. This book is a wonderful gift and legacy to leave us all. Highly recommended."

—Damh the Bard

"Ivan fully lived and embodied the Spirit of the Lord of the Dance and the Greening Power of Nature, and his joyous creativity is a testament to the simple wisdom and truth at the core of his beliefs, practices, and teachings. I commend Ivan to anyone who would dance with the sun and the moon and the web of the world and find joy there."

—Dr. Patrick MacManaway, author of *Dowsing for Health, Cultivating the Light Body,* and *Keys to Grace* and cofounder of Circles of Peace

THE BARDIC
BOOK of BECOMING

An Introduction to
Modern Druidry

IVAN McBETH

with Fearn Lickfield

Foreword by Philip Carr-Gomm

Afterword by Orion Foxwood

WEISER BOOKS

This edition first published in 2018 by Wesier Books, an imprint of

Red Wheel/Weiser, LLC
With offices at:
65 Parker Street, Suite 7
Newburyport, MA 01950
www.redwheelweiser.com

ISBN: 978-1-57863-634-1

Library of Congress Cataloging-in-Publication Data available upon request.

Cover design by Kathryn Sky-Peck
Cover photograph © Franciscah/Bigstock.com
Interior by Deborah Dutton
Typeset in Dante MT Standard, Gotham, and Boswell Regular

Printed in Canada
MAR

10 9 8 7 6 5 4 3 2 1

DEDICATION

This book is dedicated to those who are awakening to the fact that our planet Earth, potentially a paradise, is in trouble and needs help. Actually, this only applies if the term "planet" includes humans. Without humans to mess up the natural order of things, the planet would be doing very well. It is really the human race that is in trouble, and of course we can't keep it to ourselves. We spread our dis-ease around everywhere and to everything we touch. Most of the healing we need to do on the land is the result of the disharmony and damage perpetrated by humans.

Those who are moving from sleep and inertia into initiation and movement need all the guidance and encouragement they can get. Whoever you are, please realize that it is no accident that you are reading this book at this moment in time. Magic is real; there are no coincidences. We are connecting right now for an important reason.

I've come to believe that there exists in the universe something I call "The Physics of The Quest"—a force of nature governed by laws as real as the laws of gravity or momentum. And the rule of Quest Physics maybe goes like this: If you are brave enough to leave behind everything familiar and comforting (which can be anything from your house to your bitter old resentments) and set out on a truth-seeking journey (either externally or internally), and if you are truly willing to regard everything that happens to you on that journey as a clue, and if you accept everyone you meet along the way as a teacher, and if you are prepared—most of all—to face (and forgive) some very difficult realities about yourself . . . then truth will not be withheld from you. Or so I've come to believe.

Elizabeth Gilbert, *Eat, Pray, Love*

CONTENTS

Part II: The Spirit of Gaia

FOREWORD

I first met Ivan McBeth at the inaugural camp of the Order of Bards, Ovates, and Druids (OBOD) that was held in a field in Wiltshire over twenty years ago. A member of the Order had asked if he could invite a friend. This friend turned up and immediately pitched a teepee, flung off his clothes, and arranged his tent with the sides wide open, so that he could be close to the elements and the stars. What an impressive figure Ivan was—larger than life, with his smiling face and funny hat!

The next day, Ivan gave a presentation on his current project, which was working with the Marquis of Bath to build a stone circle larger than Stonehenge on the Longleat estate. Ivan seemed so free of inhibitions, such a happy person—and he was engaged in such an extraordinary project—I wanted to get to know him. We soon became friends, and he joined the Order.

Then Ivan met the friend he calls June in this book and began working with her in her grove in Bristol. It was at one of their OBOD Grove meetings, when they were building a small stone circle and finding it hard to maneuver a particularly large stone, that Ivan suggested everyone touch the stone while chanting the Awen. He had remembered the story of Merlin singing the stones into position at Stonehenge. Later, he recounted how, as they chanted, the stone began to seem lighter, and they were able to maneuver it into its socket easily. A few years later, Ivan and his partner were running four camps a year for the Order and had created a series of camps to build a huge and beautiful stone circle in Surrey. They chanted each stone into place.

It was at one of these camps that I found myself in the most surreal situation imaginable and laughing more than I have ever laughed in my life. It was a very hot day and all of the camp— perhaps a hundred adults and fifty children—were engaged in a "Wide Game" that took place over two fields. Ivan and I had been designated as "hooblies"—monstrous creatures who carried giant water pistols called Super Soakers. Our job was to cool participants down by "attacking" them—spraying them with water.

To make ourselves look as frightening as possible, we decided to cover ourselves in mud from head to foot. We submerged our naked selves into a mudpit and, as the participants began roaming the fields, smeared ourselves in brown and green slime. We needed to help each other to cover our faces while making sure none of the mud entered our eyes or mouths. We performed this service for each other, laughing so much that it seemed to take forever. When we climbed out of the mudpit, I took charge of one field, Ivan the other. I attacked a group of people—soaking them as they stood still in astonishment—only to find that they were, in fact, a group of Quakers looking for a Quaker camp that was in the vicinity. They retreated in horror to their cars, only to be attacked by Ivan with his Super Soaker as they scrambled to escape the madness of the Druids.

The Bardic Book of Becoming

When Ivan had nowhere to live, we offered him the little house in our garden, and he lived there while he wrote his first book. Again, I have abiding memories of laughter: Ivan sitting on a tin tray hurtling down the snow-covered hillside behind our house; me praying this wasn't his last moment as he sped toward the fence at the bottom of the hill; squeals of laughter as we shot at each other with BB guns in the garden; catching him trying to sneak chocolate bars out of the house under cover of darkness.

Each of us works with Druidry in our own way—that is its beauty and its gift. Unlike "organized" religion, Druidry is "disorganized" in the best possible way. When we follow Druidry, we are not in a restaurant, we are in a kitchen. We work with ingredients—perspectives, methods, exercises, and rituals—that we can combine in our own unique ways to create a Druidry that is to our own taste. In this book, you can read Ivan's own unique take on the subject.

It's up to each of us to be inspired by those who have gone before us—to use the ideas and methods they suggest that work for us and to discard those that don't. This creative, independent, empowered approach to the subject shuns dogmatism and embraces universalism and eclecticism. Long live such a free approach to spirituality, and long live Ivan's own unique vision of a Druidry for the future, inspired by the ancient past!

Philip Carr-Gomm

INTRODUCTION

I met Ivan McBeth at the American Society of Dowsers' 2004 convention in Vermont. He was teaching a day-long class about stone circles—their history, design, uses, and energetic importance. Ivan was a master stone-circle builder, who had designed and installed at least twenty-five full-sized circles around the world.

After an informative lecture and slide show, Ivan wanted us to "get it" with our bodies. He took us to a small valley where we were instructed to become a human stone circle. We anchored ourselves into our earthly positions around a chosen center point and linked our energies to contain and enliven the space between, beneath, and above us. Ivan stood to my left and asked us all to join hands. He led us in a spiral dance as we hummed, raising our voices together. Ivan called this ritual the Humming Bee or the Cosmic Orgasm!

As the second person in line, I ended up belly to belly with Ivan as the rest of the group spiraled in tighter and tighter, forming a powerful ball of energy. The humming continued to build, until the whole group let out a great cry as our crowns blasted open, sending off a wave of power and love to the whole area. Meanwhile, to my astonishment, I felt lightning bolts of energy firing between Ivan and me. I knew I liked this man a lot, but I had no idea what was happening.

A couple of weeks later, I received an email from Ivan saying his visa was running out and that he was heading back to his native England. He planned to return to Vermont the following spring and wanted to offer a shamanic healing course but needed help setting it up. Thus began our twelve-year partnership in work, life, love, and land.

The Green Mountain Druid School opened its rustic doors in the spring of 2006. In the fall of that year, we signed papers to become legal stewards of our home, school, and sanctuary, which we called Dreamland—seventy acres of rolling hills, forest, ponds, and brooks in Worcester, Vermont, complete with an out-rageous vista. I joined the first group of students to go through the three-year program, while at the same time assisting Ivan with the running of the school.

Ivan dedicated his life to the quest for freedom. For him, it was a matter of survival. He began this life feeling lost, sad, and confused about "reality." As soon as he was old enough, he began traveling around the world and immersing himself in wisdom teachings. Through this process, he transformed into a man who lived deeply, fully, wildly, and often on the edge—having many near-death experiences along the way!

Ivan's later years were dedicated to sharing what he learned with others. His teachings came from the heart, focusing on experiential learning, connection with nature, presence, commit-ment, and transformation. He continued delving, learning, and facing his own wounds as he taught his students to do the same.

As an elder, he was known for his wisdom, warmth, unshakable humor, and optimism. He truly practiced what he preached. His final passage was a glorious act of service to community and freedom from the ancestral wounding that so many Pagans carry with them.

Ivan never turned away a willing learner. When we were approached by friends in Colorado about making the teachings available to those farther away, he began writing our extensive and transformative Home Study Course. Seeing him put so much time, heart, and soul into this material, I encouraged him to share his wisdom in a broader way by writing a book. In the winter of 2015–2016, Ivan was able to return to Glastonbury, England, for a writing retreat. It was an important time for him—a time of *re-membering* his formative places, foods, people, and his spiritual home.

Ivan was a great healer and teacher for me personally, as I was for him. Like most couples, we had our struggles, but we were (mostly) willing to look at our shadows and take responsibility for our "stuff." What brought us together was a deep soulful love that reached across age difference, across lifetimes, and over a vast ocean. What brought us together was the work we were called to do for the Earth, for community, and for each other. Over the years, we developed a symbiotic and alchemical working relationship that brought forth the best in each of us.

Ivan's legacy will continue as long as people are ready to step into this magical adventure we call Druidry. He was a prolific writer, and his teachings continue to change lives here in Vermont and around the world. This book came about because of his deep commitment to this path, to the Earth, and to his students everywhere. He is still active as a teacher, guide, and healer. Don't be surprised if he shows up in your grove!

We believe that traditions need to evolve and respond to the times, the culture, and the land in which we live, or they become outmoded and die. This approach to Druidry is very alive. The next phase of my evolution begins by honoring and carrying forward the wisdom of my partner, my husband, my teacher, my beloved ancestor. I am deeply grateful to have been able to have this book published for Ivan—his long-held dream come true!

Ivan died much as he lived—in acceptance, love, and service to his community. He had built a deep relationship of respect with death, and I think it was mutual. On the morning of September 23, 2016, Ivan passed away peacefully at home. He went out like a king, engaged passionately in the preciousness of life, while fulfilling his sacred purpose right up until his last breath. He chose a time when we would both be surrounded, supported, and embraced by our loving community for three days of vigil.

At Imbolc, after eleven years of running our Druid school together, I was prepared to step in as Chief of the Green Mountain Druid Order and sole director of the Green Mountain Druid School. I carry my own special magic and inspiration, which continues to be honed by life, love, and loss. And the journey continues.

I wrote the following poem during an early phase of my grieving. I offer it here in hopes that it will give you a taste of our abiding love, our amazing community, and Ivan's profound passage.

The Cauldron of change is strong.
Forged in Her eternal flame,
It holds me as I dive deep
Into the frothing waters
Of grief and loss,

Then back into stillness, the great Mystery.
Heart cracking open, not broken,
I am transforming . . .
From caretaker to taking in care,
Refilling by the grace of many hearts and hands.
Community of love; the returning tide;
So much gratitude; I am blessed.

Harvest King, released at Equinox
From earthly struggle;
The ultimate sacrifice, you are sacred,
Gone away, yet more present than ever,
Ecstatic, free, bright, and big.
Larger than life, you are Everywhere!
More on purpose, still in service,
Grace in death, preciousness of life.
More than ever you teach us
Dance thru pain, never complain.
Sovereign Chief and Dragon Master.
Love eternal. We are One.

Fearn Lickfield, Beltaine 2017

Part I

THE SPIRIT IN YOU

Chapter 1

WE ARE ONE

We are One. Simply look out of any spacecraft window or inspect any photograph of our world taken from a satellite or space station. There is no denying it. We are One.

In fact, we have always been One. We are One now and always will be. In order to successfully witness our oneness, however, we need distance and perspective. Once we have created the correct conditions, it is there, right in front of our eyes. The body of our planet—the continents, the mountains, the oceans, the trees, the vegetation, the humans, the animals, the atmosphere, and everything that lives on, above, or below the surface of the world—is, simply, one integrated entity that has presence and consciousness. Everything is symbiotic, dependent, and interdependent. We even have a visible silver-blue aura that envelops us—the atmosphere. We are truly One.

From a holistic perspective, we are a collective consciousness spinning through the stars on an eternal journey of transformation and evolution. The Earth is alive, an awesome miracle, and you and I have been chosen to be part of that miracle. Chosen by whom or what? Who knows? We have been trying to figure that one out for millennia. Billions of organisms are receiving life—being born—every instant, and billions are letting go of life—dying—every instant, creating space for new life. Some insects live for a few minutes, some mountains for a billion years. Humans find themselves somewhere between the two.

Earth is a huge juggernaut, an awesome community of disparate, miraculous life forms spiraling its inexorable way through the Universe. It is also an incredibly sensitive and fragile symbiotic ecosystem in which every part is completely dependent on every other part. Everything on Earth is continually evolving and, although we as individuals will only be aware of the changes that happen in our own lifetimes, our children and descendants will take the torch we carry now into the future—*if* we succeed in leaving them a healthy world upon which to incarnate and live out that future. The prognosis at present, however, is poor.

In the dawn of humanity's existence on Earth, our oneness was innocent and unconscious. We were loved and supported unconditionally by our Great Mother as her cherished children. We were given everything we needed to survive and flourish in an abundant paradise; we simply had to make the minimal effort to eat well, create adequate shelters, and ensure the continuance of our species. Those were the days!

Somewhere during the process of evolution, we lost our way. In the larger context of human history, this happened fairly recently. We forgot about our connection to the Divine—to our Great Mother, to oneness—and became divided souls. We lost our original wholeness and wandered together, yet alone, on the surface of the Earth. We became disempowered, disenfranchised, living lives without full awareness or purpose, all the time yearning for something we had lost but unable to remember exactly what it was. This is where the human race finds itself at present.

Despite the problems we face, we are incredibly lucky to be alive at such a pivotal point in history. At this time, human consciousness has evolved to a point at which we have the potential to leave our unconscious, childishly destructive behavior behind us and choose to lead conscious lives that will bring us back to wholeness. This will actually manifest when we choose, finally, to wake up, as if from a bad dream, and take stock of the situation. Then, taking responsibility for every facet of our lives on Earth, we can work together as a global community to create a balanced, harmonious life that honors the spiritual and the material equally.

We mustn't allow our magic to be diminished or become distracted by the thought that individual human beings are small and powerless. The game that we often play, in which we compare ourselves to others and end up feeling unworthy, is disempowering and simply wrong. One person—a person like you or me—can change the world, especially when we perceive ourselves as indivisible from the entire planet! Humans are awesome beings whose personal power is increasing to the point at which every thought, word, and deed has a huge effect on our future. It is up to every one of us to choose, first, whether to believe in our immense power and, second, whether to put that power to use. Finally, we must choose to use that power in the most effective and empowering way.

INWARD TO HEALING AND WHOLENESS

So how do we gather ourselves and find our way back to healing and wholeness? We cannot go back to how things were, for that is the same as a baby attempting to crawl back into its mother's womb. It's simply not going to happen! What about sorting out the problems outside us and creating peace on Earth? Well, we've been trying to heal the world for quite a while, and things are just getting worse. When the fighting stopped at the end of World War I, everyone celebrated Armistice Day at the eleventh minute of the eleventh hour on the eleventh day of the eleventh month. It was the war to end all wars; we had learned our lesson and, from that time onward, peace would reign on Earth. Hmmm. It was a wonderful dream, but, unfortunately, it remains a dream.

Druids believe that the answer does not lie outside ourselves. To create world peace and heal the planet, we really need to focus *inside ourselves*. Think about it. If everyone committed to heal the Earth without also working on themselves, there would be no real change

It is fashionable at present to regard the state of the modern world as negative and disastrous, filled with incessant fighting, greed, and power struggles, scarred by genocide and the victimization of the powerless by the powerful. We are accustomed to focusing on humanity's cruelty to one another and the wanton destruction that engulfs great areas of our planet. Most of us, however, don't truly comprehend how reality *really* works. Popular understanding suggests that the material world is the real, manifest version of reality; it is the absolute truth. It is simply *there*, and we deal with it as best we can. This version of reality, however, can transform us into hopeless victims. If we live out this paradigm, we are doomed to react, endlessly, to the apparent reality of the moment. Not a very positive or empowered state of affairs.

Druids in History

The historical Druids were a class in ancient Celtic society that administered and applied the educational, medical, and judicial systems. They advised the nobility, officiated at public and private ceremonies, and practiced their nature-based religion. They were influential poets and every court had its group of resident bards that advised and entertained the king. The Christian hierarchy eventually banned the overt practices of Druidry and sent it underground. In the 19th century, Druidry reappeared in a "harmless" form that had first been initiated in the 16th century by European scholars who wanted to reclaim their Celtic heritage. Since then, it has started to remember and rediscover itself, growing in power and influence through the years.

If you're interested in the history and practices of the ancient Druids, there are numerous books to choose from. Most of it is conjecture, and if anybody tells you that they know what the ancients got up to, don't believe them. Most of the old descriptions of Druidry, like those of Julius Caesar and Pliny, are suspect and reflect superstition and ignorance. The only way to discover what the ancient Druids practiced is through a connection to the spirit of Druidry, which reveals itself through intuition.

Druids have a much more optimistic and empowering view of the world. They believe that material, or "objective," reality is the *effect* of the reality we first create inside ourselves. In other words, the reality we believe in and imagine to be true is the initial act of creation. This imagined reality is then projected outward, where it shapes the physical world. This is how the mind works. It is an occult truth that energy follows thought. In this way, we create what we believe or think, and, consequently, our experience of life is what we imagine it to be. This works because the material world is potential and malleable, until it is molded by intent or belief. Physical reality is the *final* stage of manifestation, not the first!

Once we understand this truth, *we can choose to create the reality we wish to manifest.* Now that's more like it! Druids are very careful about the reality they choose to create, because they know that every permutation and combination has very real, physical consequences. Creating your reality, or the world, is a skill like any other—practice makes you increasingly competent. Eventually, you can take great delight in creating the world of your dreams—provided that you abide by these two core truths:

- Negative projections corrupt and cause damage.

- Positive projections heal and unify.

If the world were your very own garden to cultivate as you wished, how would you design its landscape? Which flowers would you plant? What features would you create for your own pleasure and for the delight of others? When you empower yourself, you automatically become the celestial gardener of your dreams, creating the landscapes of your wildest and wisest imaginings. As gardeners-in-training, we must ask ourselves, and each other, what we have done with the garden that was entrusted to us.

I believe that the human race is in a process of transition between an original, childlike state of consciousness and a mature, evolved state in which we will take up our rightful roles as guardians and gardeners of this planet. It is high time for us to grow up, take responsibility for ourselves, and live wholesome lives based on a more enlightened understanding of the nature of reality. Druids call this the "mastery of awareness," and they devote a lot of their precious time to developing an alternative, more heart-centered and empowered way of interacting with the world. Then they design and create the gardens of their dreams!

In the beginning, God and Goddess created the original Universe. At present, at this stage of our evolution, the Divine is passing this baton on to us, and we must learn how to accept it and run with it. This is our destiny, and we are in the process of coming of age.

Before we can exercise our powers of conscious creation, however, we have new and scary challenges to face. Until now, we could relax in our innocence and trust that the Goddess, our Great Mother, would sort it all out and make everything okay. Unfortunately, we now find that our Great Mother is shooing us out of the nest to fend for ourselves. This is disastrous, because Mummy is refusing to care for us, cook for us, clean up after us. She is no longer willing to drop everything and come running whenever we call. Some of us still haven't fully realized what is happening and continue to hope that everything will soon revert to normal, that we can continue to lead our privileged lives at the center of the Universe.

It is time to wake up and grow up. Change is in the air, and we can see more and more people awakening and joining the flow into a new state of being. Although there is a less spiritual side to this change in consciousness—spawning a whole new industry that is licking its lips over the new contracts it will negotiate and all the money it will make—there is also a new feeling in the air, a new optimism. A whole new stratum of humanity is emerging that is aligned with the Sacred—one that operates on intuition and is connected by a web of magic and synchronicity. It is time!

ONENESS AND SPIRIT

I use the word "One" as a collective noun that encompasses all of existence—humans, animals, plants, trees, insects, the world on which we live, and everything that lives on, above, and under its surface. This includes the physical land, with its rocks, waters, flora and fauna, humans, houses, and automobiles. It includes our own physical lives, our corporal bodies, our minds, and our emotions. Ultimately, it embraces the entire planet Earth and our whole Universe—the solar system, planets, Sun, stars, and deep-space objects. It means, simply, *everything*.

In order to become truly a part of this oneness, we must heal ourselves. Let's be honest. The rest of creation is doing fine, or would be without human meddling, the consequences of overcrowding, and the copious waste products and pollution we humans produce. By "heal ourselves," I mean we must make ourselves whole, make ourselves sacred. Our once-healthy minds have been brainwashed to judge the material (mundane) world as evil and spirituality as good. This artificial division, created in ignorance and fear, has caused our entire experience of life to be torn down the middle, making us a schizophrenic and very unhappy race of beings.

The artificial split between Spirit and Earth—between a presumed good and evil—is the cause of humanity's greatest suffering and, in this day and age, it is as strong as it has ever been. In fact, it is the accepted way to experience life and is the rule by which most people on Earth have been programmed to live. The suffering caused by this dichotomy does have one positive aspect, however. We humans only seem to change when our backs are up against the wall and, at present, our experiences, planet-wide, are becoming unbearable. In this context, our suffering is probably the greatest motivator we have to heal ourselves.

True healing happens when the physical and spiritual worlds are experienced as two opposite poles of the same, integrated phenomenon—the miracle of life. We have been taught that humans are, first and foremost, physical beings with thoughts, emotions, sensations, souls, and spirits. For many people, spiritual awareness is the act of going to church once a week or occasionally sitting in meditation. Our physical existence is typically emphasized to the detriment of our invisible, spiritual side. When we finally understand that Spirit is our other half, our lost twin sister, no more or less important than our physical existence, we will truly have come of age.

With this new clarity, we can consciously invite Spirit to unite with us, returning us to balance and enabling all the lost, separated, and lonely parts of existence to come back together again. By dedicating ourselves to this convergence and learning how to make it happen, we will create a new awareness and purpose for humanity. We cannot wait for this to happen outside ourselves, for we will be waiting forever. The process must start within us, for only when our inner reality changes will the outer world follow. Druidry is a path that understands and practices this type of soul healing, for it has long promoted union with nature.

It must be understood that, no matter what we do, we cannot damage Spirit. It is infinite and perfect by itself. It is, rather, the sensitive, delicate Earth that suffers from separation and denial, because physical manifestation is the consequence of the *intent* that drives the process of creation. We humans have somehow snuck in between the Creator and the intended creation and have perverted that sacred perfection with our own ignorance and ubiquitous human failings.

I believe that healing the land (Earth) is the most important and wide-reaching goal for humanity in this stage of its evolution. Healing the land starts with you and me interacting with nature and enjoying the dance of life, while embraced by the collective consciousness called Gaia. It involves the study of both awareness and geomancy and integrating their principles into our day-to-day lives. When enough of us surrender our false independence, and focus our attention on the well-being of the whole, the momentum will steadily increase until all beings finally become willing members of the interconnected circle of life. At that point, we will have truly, finally, become One.

FOLLOWING THE PATH

This is a simple book. It professes only to describe the barest rudiments of the Druid path and to provide a map through the magic worlds for those who wish to develop and heal themselves in harmony with nature. To transform your life more deeply, however, you must commit yourself to serious training over the long term.

Druidry is not merely a collection of teachings and practices; it is a way of life. You have to *live* it. There are numerous versions of Druidry taught in mystery schools around the world today, from the traditional to the extremely bizarre, and the training provided by every Druid school is unique. The Druid path I present here relates directly to my personal history and the experiences that have shaped my view of the world. In particular, it reflects the various techniques, practices, and attitudes of the Green Mountain School of Druidry, based in Vermont.

The Bardic Book of Becoming

There are three grades of Druidry: Bards, Ovates, and Druids. This book is titled *The Bardic Book of Becoming*, because bards, having been initiated into the first grade of Druidry, are taking their first steps into the realms of magic and mystery. This is a long and winding path, requiring much determined effort. Bards will make many changes to their lives during their training, each one nudging them along a well-trodden path of metamorphosis, until they become full-fledged Druids. While it is impossible to include every part of bardic training here, as there is simply too much to cover in one book, I hope to offer you an all-around view of this ancient yet modern nature-based spirituality that will accurately convey what is involved in the development of a bard.

I started life as a very wounded child, unable to cope with the world. Over the years, I have returned from a frightening and very disempowered place to a world of ever-increasing inner peace and freedom. Because of my own past, I relate to life as a wonderful opportunity for people to heal and transform themselves. Through my own experiences, and having traveled the path of healing, I feel qualified to help others heal themselves.

I am a very eclectic person. In my life, I have had the good fortune to study many spiritual traditions with some very special teachers. In addition to Druidry, I have explored Buddhism, Hinduism, Christianity, Native American traditions, Core Shamanism, Toltec Shamanism, the Norse tradition, the Mayan tradition, and, not least, Ivanism—the world according to Ivan. And I have incorporated into my life and teaching every insight and technique that has helped me on my path of healing and evolution.

I am allergic to overintellectualism, yet accept that the intellect is vitally important to understanding the principles of healing and transformation. Once you understand the theory, however, you must apply it in life. No amount of talking, speculating, theorizing, or explaining will help you in the slightest. You have to actually get out there, gather your courage, make a few mistakes, stumble a few times, and do it! The lessons I have learned through spiritual exploration have influenced how I lead my life and how I teach. My students don't get any extra letters after their names or go home with a certificate. But they *do* learn to transform themselves and their lives. In so doing, they empower themselves to transform the world around them.

To become a bard, you must awaken to Spirit. When you awaken to Spirit, you learn that you are a divided being who won't become complete until you have merged and united your physical and spiritual halves and acknowledged your wholeness in both a microcosmic and macrocosmic sense. Druidry offers a lifestyle that encourages your divided halves to merge and guides you to find your rightful place as a member of one giant, symbiotic, loving community called Gaia, or planet Earth.

Druidry teaches the presence and power of Spirit and gives you the ability to do things not possible in your normal, human state of consciousness. By living in certain harmonious and healthy ways, you can attract Spirit into your life so that you can tap into the energy to change, to heal, and to make your dreams come true. Many of the techniques Druids practice are concerned with slowing down thought processes and aligning with the speed of nature. This is because our chattering, noisy minds create so much static that there is no space left for Spirit. Once you empty your mind and create glorious silence, Spirit can enter your life.

This requires awareness—awareness of how reality works, of how love enriches, and of how dreams can come true. When you become truly aware, you understand how you fit into the scheme of things; you understand what it is all about; you understand how you can contribute to the transformation of the world. In chapter 6, we'll discuss how you can discover who and what you truly are, and then embody it.

As you begin the process of awakening, you are faced with a fundamental decision. Do you want to let your life continue on as it is? Do you want to remain comfortably numb? Or do you want to change? Do you want to become an empowered, free being? And if you choose to change, how far along that road are you willing to travel? The process of going inside yourself and exploring your inner worlds is called journeying, and this is an important part of becoming a bard. There are whole universes within to explore and enjoy! In later chapters, I give detailed instructions on how to journey successfully and reveal how simple and fun it can be.

The Druid path is charted by ritual and ceremony. These are important tools with which you can attract Spirit and learn how to affect change in your life, as well as in the world. Even though most Druid orders (communities) are unique, they all share a body of ritual and ceremony. Once you learn these, you will feel at home with most Druid groups around the world. We'll look at these practices in chapter 7.

Another important step in becoming a bard is gaining an appreciation of the true nature of creativity. Inspiration and orig-inality are considered sacred in Druidry—equal to ceremony, meditation, or healing. As you walk the Druid path, you will learn to spend a larger portion of your life exploring and sharing your inner beauty. In chapter 9, you'll learn how creativity can play a large role in your life as a bard, and how rewarding it can be to join with others, everyone expressing themselves and having fun through story, poetry, music, and dance. Through the medium of dance, you can bring meaningful movement into your life. When you learn to express yourself, warts and all, on a journey into authenticity and empowerment, you discover what joy it is to be alive and to express yourself without fear!

Once you have changed your relationship with yourself through awareness and creativity, and learned how to express that in ceremony and ritual, you can change your relationship with life. You can transform your life from a safe, habitual existence into a magical adventure. Of course, we all have to earn the money to eat, but that is no excuse to get stuck and become boring! Chapters 11 and 12 will show you how, once you have prepared and gathered your magical tools, you can enter through a magical gateway into a Hero's adventure to find your soul.

Another important aspect of Druidry is geomancy—the art of communicating and interacting with the spirit of the Earth, Gaia, the Great Goddess. Bardic training opens up magical communication with nature and takes you from so-called normalcy to a direct interaction with the world as a natural, magical being. In fact, becoming a bard is the process of creating a "new normal" that allows you to interact and communicate with all the Earth's elements in a unique and creative way.

The four elements—Earth, Water, Air, and Fire—comprise the foundation of our physical world, and you need to understand them in order to build a strong, balanced life on Earth. As a Druid, you must strive to study the individual elements in four different ways:

1. By understanding them on an intellectual level

2. By observing them in your own life

3. By interacting with them through ceremony

4. By gaining valuable practical experience with each
   element

We'll explore this process in part 2 of this book.

Hopefully, these discussions will awaken within you an understanding of a new, exciting relationship with Earth. I also offer you various techniques to facilitate your exploration of, and eventual merging with, the Earth. The greatest and most effective technique of all, of course, is love.

As you follow the path to becoming a bard, you will encounter many questions: How can you learn to understand, love, and recognize the world as a unified, sentient being? How can you create a loving and empowering relationship with her? How can you harmonize with her so completely that you merge with her? I hope that, by the end of this book, you will be able to answer some of these questions for yourself. The success you have along the path depends, naturally, on the effort you are willing to make.

Chapter 2

THE DRUID PATH

The Druid path is a way of life. All our studies, beliefs, inner real-izations, and life experiences are integrated into our thoughts, words, and actions. All Druids wish to see in the world, they strive to make happen themselves through their lifestyles, in their own lifetimes. In other words, Druids walk their talk. As Druids, we are not perfect. In fact, sometimes it is an awareness of our faults and wounding that drives us along our path.

Druids know that the seeds of their eventual healing and empowerment lie in facing and dancing with their afflictions. Our wounds lead us to healing and enlightenment. Instead of perfection, Druids strive to be *impeccable*. Impeccability is a par-ticular type of relationship between yourself and the world, in which you try to do the best you possibly can with the resources available in the moment. In this sense, Druidry is all-inclusive; nobody can be perfect, yet everybody can be impeccable!

Druidry is a path along which any person can journey. It is nondogmatic, in the sense that there is no central book or compilation of teachings that must be followed—either literally or figuratively. The test of true Druids lies in their behavior and the quality of their relationship with life. A Druid can believe in a god or a goddess, or a god *and* a goddess working together, or no deity at all. What refreshing freedom! In general, Druids deeply love nature (which includes humanity), are on a path of growth and transformation, and strive to experience divinity, or the Sacred, directly, without a go-between like a priest or a minister.

At our current stage of evolution, the human race is in the process of coming of age, and our all-loving Mother is gently pressing us to leave the safety of our familiar nests in order to learn how to fly by ourselves. She is not being cruel; she is merely attuned to the natural flows of life and wants to create the optimum conditions for the ongoing development of her children.

But let's face it. In nature, a large proportion of fledglings don't make it, and we are scared. We are leaving the blissful safety of our Mother's all-encompassing arms to go on an adventure to find our wholeness and authenticity—the beings we always were. Yet it is difficult. The great psychologist and philosopher Carl Jung calls this process "the journey of individuation."

Our task in this new stage of human evolution is to leave the unconsciousness of innocence behind and step, boldly and fully awake, into the unknown. There, individually and collectively, we will meet the unique challenges we must face to become the authentic, fully empowered beings we truly are. Life itself is our teacher. Our task, if we choose to take it, is to surrender to the flow of our lives, and to stay awake. By doing this, we will, together, recreate the paradise that was originally given to us and that we have almost totally forgotten. If we want to manifest this future, we must actively shake off the chains of inertia that we have forged through our fear and apathy.

Many people have lost their faith in conventional approaches to spirituality. Monotheistic religion doesn't do it for them anymore. They are looking for a healthier alternative with an emphasis on living in harmony with the planet and with each other, bringing the Sacred into their lives in a practical way, and finding an active spiritual community with which to share their journey. In this modern era, with climate change, uncontrollable pollution, the destruction of the world's forests, and the deep unhappiness of many people, Druidry can provide answers. It is a type of spirituality whose time has come, because it addresses all these issues in a personal, as well as a planetary, context.

Druidry is a way of life that gently leads us toward a new, healthier understanding of the cosmos. It offers a way to facilitate our transformation toward wholeness and provides a new experiential relationship with the paradise planet we have all inherited. It possesses a comprehensive living map of the inner and outer realities of the Universe in which we find ourselves, and it clarifies the complicated internal landscapes through which we all have to journey to find our true selves. Following the example of those pioneers who have walked the path before us makes it much easier to find the way to our goals.

OUT OF THE UNKNOWN

The study of awareness is very important to Druids, for it clarifies what life is all about, increases our capacity for living, and makes everything much more fulfilling. Bards are taught that reality can be likened to an iceberg. We think of an iceberg as an island of floating ice. In actuality, however, by far the greater volume of ice is invisible below the surface. Reality, according to Druids, consists of the visible ice, plus the ice below the surface. The ice floating on the surface of the sea represents something Druids call *apparent reality*, because this is what reality appears to be. If the visible ice is the known and the invisible ice the unknown, the task of Druids is, through personal experience, to transform the unknown into the known and eventually achieve the cherished state of total awareness, or enlightenment.

Exploring the unknown is never comfortable. When we leave the familiar behind, new experiences arise and enter our awareness. These experiences are often extremely challenging. Our familiar, safe boundaries expand, and we encounter events and states that we once found too scary and unacceptable to face. The fact is that we can only truly learn and transform ourselves if we leave our familiar, safe reality behind, burn our bridges, and journey through the unknown on a magical adventure to find our true selves.

Because our spiritual selves contain life, the Universe, and everything else, by fulfilling the invitation to "Know Thyself" we can connect with the infinite and the Divine. The basic requirement for this self-knowledge is ultimately very simple. We must wake up and live in the present moment. There are no exceptions to this rule.

Druids understand the final goal of their training to be the harmonious merging of Spirit and the body, or the union of Heaven and Earth inside themselves. Historically, this important spiritual event was called the Mystical Marriage. Today, it has become a walking, talking sacred space immersed in the eternity of the present moment. This is what Druids strive to make happen in their lifetimes. First it has to happen within; then it happens automatically in outer reality.

In order to bring this dream to fruition, we must make our level of consciousness fully inclusive. In other words, we must balance our empowerment with humility. I do not mean false humility, which is merely being clever with words. True humility is the knowledge that all things are equal—from a stone, to a bird, to a king, to a poor man, to a grain of sand. Another way of saying this is that Spirit is equally contained inside everything. Awareness of this truth ensures that power is used only for the right things, in the right way, at the right time.

Druidry is no glamorous circus act; it entails no hurling of lightning bolts to smite enemies. It is simply the practice of developing our characters until they flower into full authenticity and freedom. Magic is a by-product of opening our energy channels to the natural flows of the Universe. When Druids attain a high level of awareness, they become powerful beings and, at the same time, servants in service to all other beings. In truth, everything, including humans, is equal to everything else. The Mayan greeting *Inlakesh!* says it all: "I am another you!"

BECOMING ONE WITH NATURE

Druidic training consists of a combination of two main topics: awareness and geomancy. Awareness is the art of mastering the different levels of reality. An empowered Druid is someone who can change consciousness at will. Such a magician can be described as being fully awake, authentic, and in the present moment.

Geomancy is simply divination using the medium of the Earth. In modern parlance, it may also mean building a meaningful and spiritual relationship with the spirit of the Earth. Druids study geomancy in order to learn how to communicate with nature and the spirit of the Earth. The Earth is understood to be a single, integrated, sentient being—Gaia; everything on, in, or above her surface is one with her. The Druid's ultimate goal is to unite with the Earth and travel with her through eternity.

Geomancy

The Chinese practice of *feng shui* is an Eastern equivalent of geomancy that has gained wide acceptance in the West for the simple reason that it works—and often with dramatic effects. It derives from a philosophical system of harmonizing with the surrounding environment. Feng shui considers architecture in metaphoric terms of "invisible forces" known as *qi* that bind the Universe, Earth, and humanity together.

Historically, feng shui was widely used to orient buildings—often spiritually significant structures like tombs, but also dwellings and other structures—in an auspicious manner. Depending on the particular style being used, an auspicious site could be determined by reference to local features like bodies of water or stars.

Druidry can be understood as a way of life that deepens our knowledge and increases the quality of our interactions with the wonderful planet onto which we have incarnated. Like cultivating the affection of a lover or best friend, we must learn to love nature as it is, respect its integrity, explore its beingness with tenderness and curiosity, and actively care for it. Druids ask: If we are One with nature, then what is our role? Over time, as we gently transform into the living answer to this question, everything reveals itself.

When you focus your attention on nature, nature in turn becomes aware of you and intuits your intent. If your motivation is pure, nature will guide you on a magical journey of exploration and discovery, revealing herself to your thirsty eyes. This interaction creates deep bonds and helps you to increase in both awareness and natural wisdom. True surrender and service to the spirit of the land results in sovereignty. Simply admiring her beauty is a great way to open up communication with the Earth. Once she becomes aware of your love and interest, she returns her love to you in manifold ways.

The planet is sentient. As you extend your awareness deeper into nature, she reciprocates. Once she recognizes that you are serious about getting to know her better, she starts to reveal more of herself to you. You start to notice details that you missed before. Synchronistic events appear increasingly often in your life, and you are filled with surges of new energy. You feel more balanced, connected, and grounded. You develop deeper and more intimate relationships with other people and with yourself. You feel more authentic and alive.

DRUIDIC TRAINING

A Druid's training used to last twenty years and included a lot of memorizing, as it was an oral tradition, and recording of any sort was forbidden. Today, such focused commitment is extremely rare, as the conditions are different in this modern day and age. Druidic training, as practiced today, is really only an introduction to the subject and acts as a foundation upon which to ground further study. Druids who have undergone a period of formal training can then continue their studies by transforming their lives in accordance with their internal changes. In fact, their training never actually ends.

Each grade of Druidry—Bard, Ovate, and Druid—is a necessary stage in the magical development of an empowered Druid. Each embodies a unique type of energy, perception, and flavor. Each has a particular mythical being that guides students through three corresponding states of consciousness: the Magical Child comes out to dance with bards; the Hunter instructs ovates; and the Spiritual Warrior leads full-fledged Druids to freedom.

Bards

Bards learn the mysteries of the heart. By contacting and activating their inner Magical Child, bards emerge from years of habit, heaviness, and armored seclusion and learn how to play. They spend time in circles with like-minded others who also wish to explore the bardic realities. They gather their courage and determination and learn how to relax and reveal their true selves, warts and all. They choose a medium through which to express their creativity—one or more of the bardic arts, such as storytelling, poetry, dance, music, or song. They encourage inspiration to arise within themselves. They learn how to communicate, and master the art of expressing themselves clearly, while accurately understanding others.

Bards-in-training learn how to move their bodies with grace and authenticity by practicing sacred dance. They develop their voices and study the power of the Word. They learn the foundations of Druidic magic and are introduced to ceremonies, rituals, altars, and the power of nature. They lighten up their lives and commit themselves, in ceremony, to enter on magical adventures to liberate their souls.

The Bardic Book of Becoming

Ovates

By contrast, ovates learn the mysteries of the mind. Having completed the bardic grade, newly initiated ovates focus on mastering the principles of awareness, healing, and self-transformation. Bards sit around a fire with other Magical Children playing, making music, and expressing their creativity; ovates walk into the deep forest alone after sunset to face and dance with their shadows. There, they explore and heal their wounding and build new, healthy relationships with life and death.

Ovates face their fears and empower themselves. They strive ceaselessly to still their thoughts and learn how to access silence—the energy of the Sacred. They understand with their whole being that life is a mystery, and they consciously enter that mystery. In doing so, they become part of it. Ovates make a commitment to accept and honor the uncomfortable realities of life equally with the pleasurable—the dark with the light. Their goal is self-transformation.

Ovates develop their magical powers and learn to master their will through harvesting, preparing, and learning how to use a wand. Their role model is the Hunter, and they learn that the only way to facilitate self-healing and transformation is by hunting and trapping the extra energy needed to generate meaningful change in their lives. They develop their intuition, become increasingly aware of the invisible worlds, and build relationships with magical helpers. Ovate training is extremely hands-on, involving experiences of shamanic death, symbolic burial, and conscious entry into a new incarnation. Ovates then empower themselves by facing their fears and doing the impossible. They walk on fire.

Druids

The third and highest grade of Druidry builds on the first two. Druids learn the power of intent. In the Druid grade, the skills and transformations of the Bardic and Ovate grades are integrated into the initiates' everyday lives, engendering simple being and authenticity. Those who have achieved the Druid grade have awoken; they have created a new, positive way of interacting with life. They dedicate themselves to becoming forces for healing in the world by creating sacred space and allowing their presence to bring blessings wherever they go.

If so moved, these initiates become spiritual leaders in their communities and develop their roles as priests or priestesses, officiants, healers, and teachers. They learn how to uphold the principles of justice, help to resolve conflicts, and practice the art of peacekeeping.

Druids develop their powers of healing, teaching, and creating sacred space, and take action whenever they deem it necessary. As they gain experience, they become increasingly skilled in creating and changing the world about them in both the visible and invisible realms. They become fonts of experience and wisdom and make themselves available as resources to their fellow Druids and their communities. At the same time, they increase their loving relationship with nature, which responds in kind, revealing secrets to their blossoming awareness.

The role model and archetype of the Druid grade is the Spiritual Warrior. While the Hunter hunts and acquires excess energy, the Spiritual Warrior puts it to use by acting in the world with growing authenticity and power through a technique called *not-doing*. Where *doing* is living life in a familiar, habitual way, *not-doing* is the practice of consciously changing habits and accustomed, energy-draining conduct and substituting more healthy, energy-rich behaviors. The tool of a Spiritual Warrior is *impeccability*, which means not perfection but doing the best possible with the resources available in the moment.

It is a great achievement to complete all three grades of Druidic training, for it demands constant, determined effort over a long period of time. Moreover, a Druid's commitment is always tested, so it demonstrates great strength of character. The graduates of the Green Mountain School of Druidry celebrate their achievement by spending two weeks on a pilgrimage through southwest Britain, visiting ancient and modern sacred sites, and finally performing a marriage ceremony to unite with the land inside the hanging stones of Stonehenge.

If you decide to investigate Druidry, the only way to give it a fair chance is either to enter authentic Druidic training or to commit yourself to practice it at home for a suitable length of time. A year and a day is a magical period of time to give it a fair trial and should be sufficient to recognize any benefits or changes in yourself that occur as a result of your practices. I emphasize that Druidry is not merely an intellectual exercise but a path to transform *your entire life* into a practice of impeccability and power. If you feel ready to give Druidry a try, read through this book thoroughly, and then begin to practice its lessons in a disciplined fashion.

A daily spiritual practice is essential for any meaningful growth to occur, so set aside twenty minutes at the start of each day to devote to your practice. In addition, set aside an hour every week to study Druidry, preferably at the same time on the same day and, if possible, in the same place. Nature is the best teacher and therapist, so choose a place where you can walk, explore, and get to know her to your heart's content.

LIVING AS ONE

The Druid path is one of challenge and struggle. To some extent, we are all slaves to our own cultures, our own social conditioning, and our own internal makeup. To Druids, however, this long-term slavery is intolerable. They strive to find ways to fight for their freedom, for freedom will not simply be given to us on a silver platter. Druids study what freedom truly is, get to know themselves inside and out, then make a strategy to liberate themselves.

The Druid's task today is to do whatever is necessary to realize wholeness and regain the oneness that is our birthright. Every shred of Druid wisdom is designed to midwife this awesome reality into existence. Our true nature as human beings is to stand upright on our own two feet, connecting Above and Below. We are bridges, like trees, spanning the abyss between Heaven and Earth. As functioning bridges, every act we perform, every word we speak, and every thought we think must be dedicated to free movement between Spirit and Earth. Every action we take must be aimed at singing our souls, and the soul of our beautiful world, back home.

Reading this book—or any book—is only a superficial way of studying Druidry. Meaningful change requires commitment and action, because true transformation only happens when you decide to take life on fully, with passion and without reservation. You must accept life as it is, warts and all, and learn to dance with your shadow as well as with the light. This rarely happens by accident!

Total immersion in life is the only way to become whole. Spending time in a monastery will help to clarify and quiet the mind, but then you must own your newly won skills by putting them into practice in the world. While this book may gain your attention and, hopefully, inspire you, the work of transformation will only start when you commit yourself to rigorous training, and then apply that training by getting your hands—and the rest of your physical and energetic body—seriously dirty!

The planet and all our fellow human beings are going through some tough times, and the best antidote to this suffering and confusion is awareness and coming together in groups and community. The Hopi Indians are very clear about what can save us and the planet Earth. Their advice is for us to live in community, pooling our resources so that we can act in unison with others. The time for the lone wolf is over. We can only succeed together, and this will require right relationship and good communication skills. We need to get our priorities straight. We must also ask ourselves the following questions:

- Where am I living?

- What am I doing?

- What are my relationships?

- Am I in right relation?

- Where is the water supply?

And we must do the following things:

- Establish a fruitful garden

- Speak our truth

- Create community

- Be good to ourselves and to each other

- Don't look outside ourselves for a leader

Wise words indeed.

Trained Druids are empowered beings. As such, we learn to manifest the dreams of our hearts. Power means, literally, *the capacity to act*. We use our power to do good and wholesome deeds, because it feels so much better than using our power for harm. And what a joy it is to embody our authentic selves fully and to live the life of our hearts' desires! This is our vision; this is our yearning; this is why we struggle with so much determination and courage to create our freedom. This is how we repair the tear in the fabric of existence, for we are truly One with all beings and all things. May our heartfelt efforts finally result in bringing our own souls and, subsequently, the soul of our wonderful planet, back home.

Blessed be!

Chapter 3

REBIRTH INTO SPIRIT

There came a time in my life when I arrived, guided by forces completely out of my ken, at Nuweiba, a coastal oasis on the Gulf of Aqaba on the east side of the Sinai Desert. I found myself being assimilated into a thriving, vibrant international community that lived on and around a huge sand dune that was called, appropriately, the First Dune. The eclectic group of people who inhabited the First Dune were primarily adventurous and dedicated world travelers. Nuweiba was a paradise in the exotic realms of the Middle East where tuned-in travelers could rest, recuperate, relax, and have magical adventures of the best kind.

As I settled into my new home, I took in my surroundings. The sand was a white powder that felt soft on the skin. It rolled in huge dunes along a coastal strip from Eilat in the north to Ras Muhammad in the south. It surged inland like a solid sea until it hit a range of yellow-brown mountains that separated the coastal plain from the interior. The Sinai is primarily a mountainous desert interspersed with sandy areas. If you know where and how to look, however, beautiful sweet water is never very far away.

The Gulf of Eilat sparkled azure blue in the sunlight. A hundred yards off the coastline, there is one of the most famous and beautiful coral reefs in the world. From its colorful, protective abundance, the beach community caught a lot of its food, and I experienced hours of pleasure cruising slowly over forests of gently waving and darting sea life with a borrowed snorkel and mask. On the far side of the water towered the mountains of Saudi Arabia. At sunset, the dying Sun kissed them, making them glow in vibrant maroons and crimsons, which were then reflected off the still mirror of the water in a riot of color that gave the Red Sea its name.

A collection of strange and wonderful dwellings had sprung up out of the sand, made with love, caring, and incredible creativity by the itinerant travelers. They were variously fashioned from cardboard, blankets, driftwood, and old tents, providing the owners with all the protection they needed from the elements in the Sinai. As a rule, the worst they needed to withstand were the sandstorms that occurred early each year. Seasoned travelers knew to bring sturdy goggles as eye protection and a silk scarf to wrap around their mouths and noses as a filter when the air was filled with dust and sand particles. As for waterproofing—on average, there is usually only one day of rain per year in the Sinai.

An important part of the Nuweiba colony's magical allure was the fact that it was dedicated to naturism. A large proportion of its inhabitants lived and went about their business completely naked. It was delightful, refreshing, exciting—and terrifying. The Israelis called these eccentric desert dwellers *nudistim*. The natural casualness of the people there and their all-over tans lent them an almost otherworldly beauty. I wished at a very deep level to attain the depth of freedom and beauty they enjoyed.

I knew instinctively, however, that the internal state of freedom and poise enjoyed by these beautiful people was only minimally dependent on physical appearance. It manifests in almost everyone who has nothing to hide and embodies a type of internal grace that is achieved only after deep self-examination and self-transformation.

When I first arrived, I had to make an immediate decision. Would I remain there and winter at the First Dune, facing my demons around exposing my body in public? Or would I leave immediately and deny the challenge that I had been given by destiny? After some soul-searching, I realized that this was no ordinary journey I was on; it was a magical adventure to find and heal myself. There was no decision to make, really, except to acquiesce to my fate. Okay then, I thought, bring it on!

I decided to stay and participate in the bizarre unfolding of both my outer and inner adventure. I was immediately thrown back to my childhood when I wouldn't go swimming with my friends because I judged my body to be fat and ugly. Along with that came the fear that I would become sexually aroused when speaking with a naked woman. And on top of *that* was the fear that people would find me lacking because my manhood was too small.

I needed a plan, and quickly! I decided that, initially, I would take off all my clothes while sunbathing; if I felt comfortable with that, I would venture naked short distances away from my home base.

Soon, I was reveling in the incredible feeling of freedom and naturalness this innocent behavior unleashed in me. Simply to feel the breeze and Sun on my sensitive naked body was enough to send me into ecstasy. Plunging into the warm azure sea unhindered by a bathing suit affected me in a deep, archetypal way. I felt myself changing at a profound level. I was tasting freedom!

I realized I had started to step out of hiding and was projecting myself, faults and all, out into the world. And, in doing so, I was starting to love and honor myself. I gave thanks for my great good fortune. My body was responding well to the Sun and the white bits were slowly but surely transforming themselves into an unblemished bronze. I felt beautiful and powerful and connected to all of nature. I realized I was transforming unbelievably fast! I imagined that, had I stayed at home in the U.K., it would probably have taken me lifetimes to change so deeply and completely.

In addition, I was learning how to survive in a potentially lethal environment. Nuweiba was both delightful and ruthless. It was beautiful but also a world of scorpions, poisonous snakes, sharks, serious illness, violence, religious intolerance, terrorism, dehydration, and sudden death from a variety of unpleasant causes. I felt as if I were constantly living on the edge between life and death, and I made sure that I never got complacent. Then I realized that living so close to death was throwing me into a state of constant, heightened awareness and opening my senses to understandings and experiences not normally available in a safe, civilized style of life.

I wondered where this adventure would eventually lead me, and I was always on the lookout for omens. Living on the edge like this kept me awake and alert, like a wild animal. My intuition and dormant instincts began to sharpen. I started to become aware of little things that I normally wouldn't have noticed, both in nature and in the interactions between people. This awareness

The Bardic Book of Becoming

brought me great joy. I often sat in a comfortable vantage point overlooking the First Dune and beach, observing people and the way everything changed throughout every day. I wondered at the way my life was unfolding and how it interacted with everyone else in this magical place.

OUT OF THE SHADOWS

After I had been living in Nuweiba for about three weeks, I started to get indications of the next part of my journey. From time to time, I caught sight of some very special men and women passing through, always following the shore of the bay. I discovered that they lived roughly four or five miles to the south of the First Dune. As they walked past the community in which I lived, I watched them with a growing sense of awe and longing.

If the denizens of the First Dune were high-energy and beautiful, these occasional visitors possessed the most awesome, extraordinary presence. There seemed to be a sparkle and crackle in the air as they passed, and my body experienced a physical jolt whenever I saw them. They appeared fully naked, their skin unbroken by white lines, walking tall in their authenticity. They exuded confidence, balance, and awareness. They were fully relaxed and almost otherworldly. They appeared to me to be whole humans, radiant in their beingness—in other words, expressing their divine natures. They possessed such natural, graceful power that I called them the Gods and Goddesses.

I suddenly realized that my destiny was to become one of these magical beings. I had no doubts; I simply felt a calm certainty. My whole being yearned to undergo the experiences and healings that would bring this level of awareness into my life, yet I knew this blessed state was still many years, maybe lifetimes, away. Compared to these Gods and Goddesses, I felt very small, wounded, and unworthy. At the same time, I knew that every journey starts with a first step.

As I witnessed these enlightened, realized humans walking past my humble home, I set my intent to travel to their kingdom and enter it if I could. I recognized my introduction to Nuweiba as a unique chance to find deep healing for my soul, possibly the only real opportunity I would be given in this lifetime. My determination became focused and unbending, and I decided to do whatever I had to do to prepare for my transition into—I could only imagine what. Whatever happened, I wouldn't waste this chance; I wouldn't ignore this beckoning portal. When I was called—which I knew in my bones I would be—I determined to respond as impeccably, and as whole-heartedly, as I could.

And then the call came.

I can only adequately describe the experience by relating it as it unfolded in my consciousness:

It is approaching sunset, and I am on my way to meet my destiny. Until now, I have been sheltering on the First Dune and wrestling with an excruciating decision. Should I journey deeper into this new desert reality? Or should I leave this magical space, perhaps forever? I am so scared!

I realize that there is actually no choice to make. My spirit is finally emerging from its hiding place and is starting to reveal its true nature. I need to midwife its birth properly and impeccably. To facilitate this, I must travel deeper into the unknown.

I know that today is the day. I carry my meager belongings in my backpack and say my goodbyes to those who have given me friendship and pleasure in my time at the First Dune. They think I am crazy to leave the paradise I have shared with them and, indeed, I have no convincing explanation for why I have to travel further into the unknown.

I climb the Second Dune, a massive sand barrier dividing the beach north from south—the known from the unknown. It is the boundary between the realm of the Gods and Goddesses and the community of the First Dune. I am about to leave my petty world of ego and self-focus behind. I want more than anything else to transform and heal myself—to become, like them, a self-realized, authentic person.

I reach the top of the Second Dune, my inner bull fully activated, hot steam issuing from its nostrils. And then I hit an elastic, yet impenetrable, barrier. My inner bull shakes his head and tries again, only to be gently but firmly prevented from moving one inch beyond some sort of invisible force field. He starts to get annoyed and prepares to charge the barrier, but I step in. I realize that escalation is useless, that this invisible shield isn't going anywhere, especially with the application of force. I invite the bull back into his stable. He relaxes and starts to munch hay.

I stop, slip my backpack onto the sand, and use it as a seat. Something tells me to relax, stop pushing, and enjoy the scenery. This I do. It is so outrageously beautiful! I allow my mind to wander, and I enter a timeless zone. I sit and watch the Sun, like my former life, setting in a blaze of glory—a fitting, timely death—over the inky sea. I ponder my journey so far.

Before my arrival at the First Dune, I was a featureless, characterless person without hope or direction, floating unconsciously in the oceans of life. I knew that there was a place where I belonged but had no idea how to discover or reach it. I experienced everything in different shades of gray, and I even contemplated suicide. When I arrived at the First Dune, I experienced great excitement and promise—and unbearable fear. For better or for worse, I let go of my past and experienced a rite of passage into a new start, a new life.

There is an old shamanic saying that the Bird of Freedom travels in a straight line. If it knocks at your door, you must drop everything, climb onto its back, and accompany it. If you miss the chance, it will *fly off and never return. I feel at this moment that this liberating bird has landed right in front of me and that I have climbed onto its back. I feel a strong sense of freedom, as if I am assuming some sort of definite form and developing my own authenticity. It feels extremely exciting, exhilarating—and dangerous.*

My body is shivering—it knows exactly what is going on, even if my brain is bemused and confused. The First Dune was a plateau, a resting place where I could gather the energy for my entry into the world I always knew existed but could never find. I am now at a portal that leads from that past into my future. This point in time and space is the start of a whole new life, a life of meaning and fulfillment—and terrible danger. From this moment on, I must start to find and express my true Self, a being I have been denying until now.

As the sunset fades in the indigo sky, I look back and observe the world I am preparing to leave. I see floodlights, radiating white blinding light, scouring the desert landscape and violently dispelling the darkness. They are security lights designed to discourage terrorists from creeping up on the nearby Israeli settlement and causing mayhem. The dazzling, stark light irradiates the desert and destroys its gentle secret beauty. I know that fear is depriving the desert beings of their peace and blessed rest.

I hear loud electronic music filling the space between Nuweiba and the Second Dune, assaulting this magical landscape and destroying the natural, healing peace of the night. I sense the excessive light and sound as symptoms of the oblivion into which I had been attempting to escape. I realize that, from this moment on, this is no longer my home.

I turn toward my future. Darkness rules here; shadowy movements indicate the presence of palm trees swaying in the gentle sea breeze. Emerging stars hang, ripe in the velvet night sky, whispering messages of hope and promise. The warm breeze carries news of sand, sea, seaweed, spice, and desert life to my opening senses. This is the world of the silence, of the invisible shadow realities that demand faith and trust. This is the unknown, the darkness, the adventure that beckons, the valley of the shadow of death, the realm of the Gods and Goddesses. My heart beats strongly, and my spirit moves in the joy of its immanent becoming.

I stand up and bow to the world I am leaving. Thank you for providing me with my birth, my physical existence, my health, and the seeds of my true self. Thank you for nurturing and protecting me in the chaotic yet fertile soils of my youth. Thank you for finally leading me here to this sacred space at exactly the right time. I feel at One with the flow of synchronicity, with outrageous fortune, with everything. At One.

I turn and bow to the world I am about to enter. Oh how I have longed to find you, enter you, dance deep into your being! At last, I stand at your portal. I surrender to you, your gifts, and your pathways. Here, I meet my destiny!

I walk forward and pass through the portal. There are no more barriers, invisible or otherwise. My true life starts here, now. I suddenly notice a bright, twinkling star in front of me. It smiles lovingly and says: "If you get to know me and become my friend, you will never lose your way again."

I give thanks for my great good fortune. I am home, at last. Reborn. Blessed be!

Chapter 4

STARTING YOUR JOURNEY

Stepping onto the Druid path is a rite of passage that leads from a so-called "normal" life into a world of magic and mystery. Students whose motivation is simple curiosity or glamor will probably drop out quickly, because commitment is always tested. Only those whose vision is clear, whose commitment is strong, and who are ready to take on the challenges and gifts of the unknown will persist. It takes great courage and strength of character to drop your armor and make yourself vulnerable to the truth.

Moreover, the transition into a life of awareness and responsibility is far more effective when present circumstances are so uncomfortable that aspirants are motivated by necessity. The very best conditions for self-transformation occur when it is perceived as an act of survival, as it was for me in my journey to the Second Dune. In these extreme circumstances, there is no room for doubt or resistance, only immediate action.

If you are inspired by Druidry and feel it is the way forward for you, you must first ask yourself if you are serious. And *how* serious are you? Are you ready to commit yourself to a new path, a new life? If you feel you are ready and are prepared, then ask yourself: What am I prepared to let go of, to sacrifice, in exchange for the chance to create my own freedom?

In my teenage years, I read in some occult book that, in order to receive spiritual teachings and transform yourself, you needed an honorable purpose, which the book defined as: "I want to learn in order to serve." I was so happy! I had found the key to unlock the mysteries of life! All I had to do was find the right door! Imagine my delight when, a month or so later, I woke up inside a dream that seemed to reveal the location of the door awaiting my key.

I was walking through London in a drizzling rain early one morning before sunrise. My steps took me to a large temple-like building capped with a dome and fronted by two huge wooden doors that I immediately recognized as the portal I had been seeking for so long. In great excitement, I crossed the road and knocked on one of the doors. Massive sounds reverberated through the building, like thunder rolling into the distance. After a while, a small door in the larger one opened, and I saw a dark figure in the shadowy darkness. He asked, with a Cockney accent: "What do you want?"

I was determined not to be disappointed by this ordinary question, delivered by an ordinary sort of person who didn't recognize me as the adept I really was, so I presented the spiritual answer I had been rehearsing: "I want to learn, in order to serve."

Silence.

The infuriating voice from the darkness then asked me a completely irrelevant question: "Do you smoke?"

I replied in the affirmative.

"When you stop smoking, you can enter!" was all he said.

I hung my head in defeat. I knew I couldn't do it, because I was hopelessly addicted and didn't have it in me, at that time in my life, to stop smoking. I turned around and slunk away across the road, knowing I had failed and unsure if I would ever have another chance to find the magical portal.

On the Druid path, every aspirant is required to sacrifice something precious or difficult to relinquish to prove they are ready to enter the portal into a new life of high energy and healing. You may not be required to do this before your training starts, but the demand will come, sometimes when you least expect it. Are you ready to offer up what will be requested of you? Your sacrifice needs to be genuine, depriving you of something precious or demanding of you an effort. Some are required to leave a former life or home in order to heal and transform. Others are required to lose weight and find their health again. Still others must pay off long-standing debts. We all have individual challenges we must face or goals we must achieve in order to start on our journeys. What is your sacrifice? What is your challenge?

Although the Goddess loves you unconditionally, the God requires a sacrifice. In his view, nothing happens without payment of one sort or another. Sacrifice means, literally, to make something sacred. In other words, which of your habits or indulgences are you willing to offer as a gift to the powers that will guide you to your goal? You don't get anything for nothing. Life is an energy exchange.

COMMITTING TO CHANGE

To become a Druid, you need a teacher or a school. At the start of your evolution, you can only go so far and so fast by reading books or by receiving inspiration. There is so much to learn and to experience on this path that, eventually, you will need training that can provide you with strong foundations for your life as a Druid. To help you identify your goals and commitment, try this simple exercise:

1. Go into yourself and contemplate your desire to study Druidry.

2. Write down all the reasons you want to study. Give yourself about ten minutes, or however long you need, to do this.

3. Write down all your resistances to studying Druidry. Give yourself ten minutes, or however long you need.

4. Contemplate both lists.

Look first at all your positive reasons for studying Druidry. Are they strong enough to support you along the path and overcome your resistances?

Now look at your resistances. Are they strong enough to sabotage and obstruct your progress on the path of Druidry? How many of them are actually real? Time restraints, for instance. Time is precious and must be used wisely. Do you believe you are a spiritual person? Then what proportion of the day do you allocate to spiritual matters? Studying Druidry will probably take up, on average, forty-five minutes a day. If you are awake fifteen hours a day (sleeping nine hours), then forty-five minutes is only 5 percent of your waking life. What sort of commitment is that? Hmmm.

Money is another serious obstacle. Do you have enough money to enroll in a Druid school? If the answer is yes, no problem; do it. If the answer is no, ask your heart if you *really* want to become a Druid, an empowered magician and steward of nature. If it answers no, then go no further along the Druid path and discover what you really want to do instead. If it answers yes, then use all your energies to make it happen. Divert more money to your spiritual evolution. Know that Druidry is a serious investment in your life, as it will lead you to become an aware, empowered human being. Can you somehow make your studies cheaper? Are there any discounts available? Work exchange? Grants? Do some research, or simply start studying, if you dare! Trust, and allow the Universe to create the extra money you need. Do whatever you need to do; you'll find a way.

What about children or partner(s)? Is Druidry against your religion? Do you want to study against the wishes of your parents, or your wife, or your husband, or your friends, or your kids, or your bank manager, or your choral society, or your military unit, or your friends, or your pets? Now wait a minute. Who's in control of your life, anyway? If you think the answer is you, and you truly want a soul that is healthily connected to your body, then you've simply got to do what your heart desires, as long as it doesn't cause harm to others. Go through all your resistances now, one by one, and discover the positives that neutralize them.

If there truly seems to be no way of surmounting certain obstacles, then sacrifice them to the patron deity of Druidry! Simply let them go, let the God and Goddess deal with them, and get on with what you really want to do. Druidry is a lot about creating and fighting for your own freedom, so this can be your first challenge. Imagine what your life could be without the resistances that are preventing you from starting the spiritual development you so deeply wish to initiate!

Heart, Not Mind

When making important decisions about love or spiritual matters, always ask your heart. It knows, whereas your mind only *thinks* it knows!

INTO THE GROVE

There was a point in my life when I was in an in-between state. I had recently experienced a painful separation from my partner and was waiting for new direction. I was living in Bath, a beautiful city in Avon, England, famous for its healing hot springs—in fact, the only such springs in the U.K. A friend of mine had just opened up a New Age shop there, and I was helping him move in, stock the shelves, and open up for business.

Bath is ancient; the hot springs have attracted pilgrims and worshippers since the dawn of time. The Romans built a major temple there dedicated to the goddess Sulis Minerva, and it became an important center of healing. Bath is also famous as the site of ancient trees and as home to deep forest magic. The city abounds with fairies and nature spirits. I delighted in walking the many paths and parks of Bath, greeting these sacred beings and ancestor spirits, dancing and spending time with them.

My friend's shop was built on two levels. I served behind the counter during the day and slept upstairs at night. It was a perfect situation for me. I enjoyed my work, and I could save money as I prepared to finance the next stage of my life. I enjoyed my time in Bath yet wondered when I would receive instructions from Spirit showing me my next real home and my task once I arrived there. I hoped I would continue my work with Earth energies and the spirit of landscape.

I was relaxed and didn't have a care. Although quite a shy person, I often chatted with customers and enjoyed myself. There was a good sound system in the shop and all the latest CDs. I was in my element. Crystals of all shapes, colors, and sizes adorned the shelves and cabinets. I sometimes took them out and played with them, arranging them in patterns and mandalas, exploring how each arrangement felt while fantasizing about their effects on the world. I read many books on healing, spiritual evolution, and shamanism, adding to my knowledge. In the evenings, I walked the land, exploring the wonderful and magical beings that lived there. In this way, I passed my time, waiting for change yet making myself useful and studying. I was grateful for this amazing opportunity.

Then I met June.

June was very attractive—just over five feet tall. She had an unusual and exciting aura that filled the space around her and compelled those in the shop to take notice of her. She visited regularly and bought ceremonial supplies like incense and candles. She spoke about her frequent visits to Stonehenge and other sacred places on the landscape, doing ceremonies and building relationships with the spirit of the land. I was fascinated! We got on well, exchanging stories and simply enjoying being with one another. I spent as much time as I could with her whenever she came into the shop. I always felt a sense of loss whenever she left and looked forward to her next visit.

One fateful day, after we had known each other for a couple of months, I noticed her approaching the entrance to the shop. Although everything appeared to be normal, my intuition told me otherwise. There was something unusual going on. My senses were on full alert as she opened the door and entered. Her body language was strange; she couldn't look me in the eye and, as she approached the counter, I saw that she had one hand hidden behind her back. Suddenly, she brought her hand out from behind her and held out a rose. As I took it from her, she blurted out: "I love you!" Then she ran out of the shop.

I was left holding the rose, with my mouth hanging open and an emotional storm raging inside my paralyzed exterior. Such blissful agony! I remained in an agitated state until her next visit, when we hugged. It was an amazing hug—one in which we seemed to merge and were occupying the same space down to the last atom.

Needless to say, we became lovers, and I found out that June was a Druid. And I learned that, with the right training, both men and women could become Druids. Soon after we became partners, she hosted a "Grove" meeting at her house, and I was invited to join in. I was in awe of the people who appeared there, amazed at their general level of energy and at the love and respect they shared with one another. They were truly members of a successful spiritual community, having their own private lives and yet sharing a common path.

Passing through powerful experiences together creates strong bonding, and this Druid community had forged deep relationships among its members. Spending time with them, I could see that they actively supported and looked out for one another, often conferring together whenever one or more of them had a problem. It was a privilege and very inspirational to spend time with them. I found myself wanting to join their magical circle.

And so I did. My new friends initiated me into a new way of being—yet one that was simultaneously familiar. I started my study through a correspondence course, and I proceeded at my own pace. Although I studied alone, I met with my new family at least once a month, and I asked questions to my heart's

The Bardic Book of Becoming

content. We performed ceremonies around a fire under the trees and my soul celebrated coming home and finding my people. I didn't doubt that I would eventually receive instructions to travel to some other place on this beautiful world's surface, but I immersed myself as deeply as I could in the wonderful combination of friendship, love, and magic I had found in Bath.

I also realized that we humans rarely choose to be Druids—rather, we are chosen. Our hearts must resonate with a love of nature, a love of love, and a desire to become One with all of existence. The Goddess reaches out to those she recognizes, those who are dancing to her rhythm, and guides them into a magical circle—to teachings that inspire and lead toward the world of Druidry. She cannot force you: she can only guide you, allowing you to follow your heart and open the door to Druidry yourself. Once you enter, however, she envelops you with love and provides all you need to develop into an empowered caretaker of the Earth. In time, you become One with her.

FIRST STEPS

Once you start your training, the rules that seemed important to your old life will fade and new rules will gain in prominence. Making money, having a good career, nurturing a loving and satisfying partner, enjoying evenings out with friends, and planning ten days of vacation in a favorite part of the country will still be important to you. However, other unexpected matters will start to catch your attention. Many of the rules so carefully explained to you by your former teachers—school, church, politicians, family, doctors, and other authority figures—simply won't ring completely true or seem as relevant anymore.

You will begin to observe life more carefully and to listen more closely. You will become aware of the way people use words, how they exaggerate and lie, and how unaware they are. You will realize that unconsciousness is a presence like a dark cloud that dims the light and how most people are vulnerable to its influence. You will see how violence is suppressed but remains very close to the surface in many people.

You will start to observe your behavior in more detail, with more stringent filters. You will learn many things you had formerly missed about your own character and true motives. All those things you avoided because they were simply too uncomfortable to accept will start to pop up into your awareness. And, this time, you will greet them and ask them who and what they really are. And they will reply!

At the same time, your social skills will improve. On the one hand, you may not go out socially as often; on the other hand, you may find you are much more relaxed, can communicate more deeply, have much more satisfying interactions with others, and enjoy yourself more. It is possible that you will find yourself in a new circle of friends or a new community, learning new skills—a musical instrument, a martial art—spending more time in nature, fishing, joining a choir, learning and singing sacred songs, and so on.

We get a lot of feedback from our students about the lessons they enjoyed and those they didn't. They often tell us how we can make the unpleasant or boring lessons easier and more enjoyable. This is an attitude held by most people, who believe that life is here to make us happy. This attitude sets you up for repeated disappointment.

As a bard, however, you are no longer an "average" person, and the exercises in which we ask you to participate are for your inner development and healing. So if you are made uncomfortable by an exercise, celebrate! Your soul has shown you, in no uncertain terms, a weakness or wound that you need to address and heal to find your wholeness. Instead of avoiding it, spend *more* time with it—exploring it, learning to love and accept it, and transforming it with your love. One thing is certain; nobody heals when they hate and avoid parts of themselves.

BE IMPECCABLE

Druids give a lot of value to the concept and practice of impeccability. Impeccability is emphatically not perfection, because nobody can be perfect. If you try to be perfect, you will always end up disappointed and frustrated, just like those who believe that life is supposed to make them happy. To be impeccable is simply to do the best you can, with the resources that are available to you in the moment. Nobody can be perfect. But anyone can be impeccable.

Nevertheless, it is still very difficult to lead a fully impeccable life. It is certainly worth the effort, however, because impeccability generates a whole lot of extra available energy that you can direct wherever you want it.

If your new studies are effective, you will experience your life slowly transforming. You may even realize that your thoughts are changing. What an adventure! You will become increasingly observant, noticing many things you missed before, and your life will be full—full of surprises and vibrant. Your new awareness will bring a swelling inner abundance, deeper and more relaxed friendships, a new community of like-minded people, and more enjoyment of simple things. Your life will blossom into greater depth and momentum.

The bottom line is that your journey on the Druid path must be initiated and governed by your heart. If you are faced with decisions concerning your life, ask yourself this simple question: Does this option have heart? In other words, is this what my heart really wants? If not, keep searching. If so, then shift Heaven and Earth until your wish has manifested into your physical life. Viewed in this way, life actually is incredibly simple, as it has no options!

Welcome to Druidry.

Blessed be!

Chapter 5

BECOMING A BARD

Becoming a bard requires extraordinary motivation and commitment. In ancient times, it took twenty years of training. Bards-in-training forge deep and magical relationships with the Goddess—also called the Muse—and, through their actions, gain access to her blessings. Bards consider their creativity to be a magical gift, which, with the support of the Goddess, can be developed without limit. Bards are associated with creativity, especially poetry, storytelling, and music. William Shakespeare, whom some consider the greatest and most famous poet who ever lived, is known as The Bard.

Bards can be men or women of any religion, belief, race, or color. They are associated with the Fool in the tarot—a youth setting out on a magical journey with trust, innocence, and wonder. The Fool's whole life stretches ahead of him—provided that he survives! He is, like most of us, at least partially unconscious and unaware of his surroundings as he walks his path. His face bears an optimistic, innocent, and naive expression as he blindly walks close to the edge of some very steep cliffs. In some tarot decks, a small dog accompanies him, barking and nipping at his ankles. This dog represents the Fool's undisciplined mind and rampant emotions, which distract him, pulling his attention away from the present moment.

A bard is essentially a Magical Child, exploring the Universe, playing and discovering to his or her heart's content. Bards are looked after and supported by the Great Mother Goddess, who bathes them in her unconditional love. They are partially unconscious, have not yet discovered their authenticity, and do not really understand the concept of taking responsibility for themselves.

Bards are especially dedicated to Gaia, whom they recognize as the Source of everything, including their own well-being, nourishment, safety, shelter, clothing, home, and sense of self and belonging. They care deeply for their Mother, directing love and devotion toward her. They grieve when she is hurt or damaged in any way. By celebrating the changing of the seasons and other cycles of nature, bards align themselves with Gaia on her evolutionary journey through the Universe.

SEEKING COMMUNITY

Bards primarily learn to relax and enjoy life. They learn how to interact singly and in group situations, exposing their inner selves—the good as well as the bad—in public. This ability is vitally important in the process of getting the creative and heart juices flowing, but very few individuals are born with it in this modern world. Instead, much of our vital energy is consumed in defending and armoring ourselves against the nasty "outside world" that we feel is out to get us.

The Bardic Book of Becoming

Our parents, teachers, and "elders and betters" have taught us that the world is a scary place from which we must protect ourselves at all costs. Although this is partially true, the world is also ready to welcome us into magical adventures, friendships, and fun. The trouble arises when we armor ourselves against the cruel and dangerous "stuff," because the walls we build also keep out the good and pleasurable experiences.

Bards therefore look for groups or communities that observe a way of life similar to their own. If they are successful in their quest and it feels comfortable, they join it. They surrender their own personal, isolated space and allow others in, in small yet manageable doses. They learn ways in which to connect with people by interacting as equals with the individuals of their community. Learning and sharing the bardic arts is a perfect way to facilitate this. Trust and innocence are their tools, and spontaneous expression is the reward they glean from their efforts.

Learning how to take your place as an equal among members of a group or community is a wonderful way to loosen up, diminish your ego, and experience your humanity. The Hopi Indians are very clear about this. They admonish their so-called "civilized" brothers and sisters that their strength and their great potential lies in community. Such wisdom! How else can we learn to be human, other than by interacting with others and finally becoming One with them? We must learn to be patient yet persistent, however, for the process of humanization can take a long time.

Bardic training opens the heart and grounds students at the same time. The more your heart opens, the more you will need grounding to retain your balance. Both these conditions are necessary to prepare students properly for the Ovate mysteries, which involve expansion of consciousness and self-transformation. Without a bardic foundation, a healthy and meaningful Ovate experience is not possible.

Bards learn to communicate in a compassionate and non-violent way. Much of our daily communication is aggressive, passive-aggressive, self-centered, unconscious, derogatory, discriminatory, and unfeeling. The art of "spin," so prevalent in our modern world, is a powerful tool used by politicians, the military, and people in authority to obscure the truth. This is not a good foundation upon which to relate in a heart-centered way. Bards open up respectful, loving interaction between themselves and with others, to build trust and meaningful win-win relationships. Again, this practice takes a long time to integrate into your life, but once it is set up, it can transform your communication skills and your enjoyment of life immensely.

MAGICAL ENERGY

Magic is energy from another dimension or alternate reality that breaks through into our normal perception of the world. This alternate reality is often more powerful than our familiar experience of life, and it usually appears to us as something extraordinary or magical. Magic is an important part of Druidry, and bards are instructed to set up and manage both their behavior and their beliefs in such a way as to attract it into their lives.

These high-energy eruptions into everyday reality can and do happen relatively often. They must not be regarded, however, as some sort of superpower that makes the person experiencing the phenomenon in any way special, for this merely feeds the ego and pulls us away from the Earth. As long as we consider magical events as harmless by-products of our increased life force, they are an indicator of progress in the training.

These eruptions of magic need *earthing* to make them useful to Druids. Too much magic and too little groundedness results in students becoming too "spaced out" and, in worst-case scenarios, can cause mental illness. On the other hand, too much groundedness and too little magic results in timidity, monotony, and stagnation. Bards understand the importance of balance in their magical lives and strive to cultivate it.

Each of the three grades of Druidry has a corresponding type of magic. As students progress through the grades, they learn to perceive life from three very different perspectives that when integrated, provide a rich, three-dimensional experience. The Bardic Mysteries state that magic is a product of awareness and timing, or the state of being "in the flow" of life, which is greatly enhanced by the presence of the Awen or Spirit. Like any other skill, progress in magic is made through practice, practice, and more practice!

MAGICAL JOURNEYS

Journeying is introduced to bards early in their training. This is a practice that enables them to explore their inner lives and develop their intuition. Intuition is the transrational sense humans use to perceive the invisible component of life. It manifests through our feelings, the sensations we feel on the surface and inside our bodies, and our imaginations. Bards learn how to journey in easy steps. As their abilities increase, so do the depth and degree of the journeys they undergo.

Intuition is the sense especially attributed to the Magical Child. Before it is fully developed, however, it is easily overwhelmed by our inner adult rationality. Therefore, in bardic training, our boring and responsible inner adults are initially requested to go take a hike during the time our Magical Children first come out to play. Once the inner child has gained experience and confidence, it can learn to work in harmony with its inner adult, creating a strong and magical internal partnership. In this sort of experienced teamwork, the adult holds the space safe and without distraction, while the child journeys freely through the inner landscapes.

One of the first journeying tasks bards are set is to find and create their own inner sacred grove. A sacred grove is, literally, a circle of trees that, by its very nature, is a powerful, living, sacred space. These groves are places in which Druids gather and worship. Bards are taught to create, in their imaginations, internal sacred groves that grow incrementally over time. Sacred groves are very individual and contain the energies, objects, symbols, and entities that generate the Sacred for each specific bard. These qualities are all heart-centered, and their presence creates a space where the soul of the bard can emerge into a safe and nourishing environment.

Bards visit their sacred groves often and, as they develop and change, so do their groves. It is extremely beneficial to have an active sacred space radiating from your heart, because it deeply affects your relationship with the world. Before you make a journey, or before working magically, you must first enter your sacred grove to relax, prepare, and then enter the appropriate state of consciousness. This internal sacred space is an essential resource that is used extensively in Druidry.

Gazing is another technique used by bards to awaken and expand their intuition and facilitate magical journeys. Bards learn to change the focus of their eyes to "wide-angle" vision. In doing so, they become aware of different, alternate realities. Throughout their training, they gaze at different objects in order to expand their consciousness. Some examples are fire, water, distance, snow, clouds, and trees, although you can really gaze at anything. Gazing, like many magical techniques, is cumulative. Although it may often seem as if nothing is happening, if you keep practicing, you can reach a critical mass with dramatic results!

Bards deeply appreciate and celebrate all facets of nature, a word that, for them, means "that which has been born or created." Bards believe that all things—organic and inorganic—are conscious and need to be treated as equals and with respect. It is sometimes difficult to regard humans as part of nature, but, in fact, we are also part of the great, indivisible Wheel of Life. As bards increase in awareness, nature reveals herself correspondingly, and they begin to realize the incredible miracle of which they all are a part.

The sacred archetype bards explore and work with is the Magical Child, which is the active expression of our souls. Your Magical Child lives in your heart and expresses itself in the world through open-heartedness, play, and spontaneity. This joyful child's imagination is in a constant state of creation; everything it does is authentic and original.

Magical Children are still connected to the Source of all things. They are free beings who, despite past trauma, remain intact and unwounded. They take delight in, and become empowered by play; the seriousness expressed automatically by most adults stifles and injures them. Magical Children—we all have one in residence in our hearts—are protected by their natural innocence and trust and are guided by Spirit. Bards learn ways in which to entice and encourage their inner child out to play; this is greatly enhanced by having other Magical Children to play and grow up with.

INNER CREATIVITY

Bards are best known for their creativity, even in the conventional world. Accessing their inner creativity and expressing it can happen naturally or with discipline and formal teaching—or perhaps a bit of both, depending on each individual bard. The task of the bard is to open the doors of the heart and midwife acts of creation into the world.

The bardic arts are writing and reciting poetry, storytelling, music-making, singing, acting, dancing, communicating, sharing, and play. Bards train themselves over many years to increase their artistic skills to the point of changing consciousness—theirs, as well as others'—at will. Their intent is to bring the Sacred into the world by creating magical experiences and deep meaningful interactions that result in transformation for themselves and others.

The spark of creativity smolders in our hearts—the point at which we are connected to the Source of all. This spark is waiting to ignite. All poets and writers pray that their Muse, Awen, or inspiration will bless them, open their hearts, and activate the flow of creativity inside. This muse is the female principle of the Universe, the Goddess of the Druids, who brews the sacred Awen (the energy of inspiration) in her cauldron, or womb. Therefore, to Druids, each act of creativity—whether a poem, a sculpture, or a song—is divine and sacred.

Central to the bardic experience is holding and nurturing the belief that the acts and fruits of creation are sacred. It is obvious, really. What best demonstrates the most powerful act of divinity? Creation! Bards learn that we all have a resident god or goddess that lives within us whose task is to activate our own creative power, open up and prepare our inner channels to handle the flow, and to bring beauty, creativity, and healing wherever we go.

True creativity is an act of birth, in which something is brought into existence that didn't exist before. Isn't this a miracle? We humans give birth to many different things—from physical children, to songs, to poetry, to concepts, to explanations of the Universe, to medical discoveries, to new states of consciousness, to space travel, and on and on. Consequently, Druids recognize divinity in each human being. This concept is not limited to Druidry but shared by many different cultures. Take, for example, the traditional Hindu greeting, *Namaste*, which is typically translated as "I recognize the Divine within you" or "I salute the Divine within you."

Actually, *everything* is sacred to Druids—the whole spectrum of existence, from birth to death, peace to war, day to night. However, there are some qualities expressed by humans that are considered particularly blessed and that attract the Awen— the attention of the God and Goddess—in a special and powerful way. These qualities are gratitude, courage, prayer, offering, creativity, and eloquence. Practicing any of these opens us up to channel the Sacred.

THE GODDESS

The Goddess presides over the Bardic grade. Bards are her Magical Children, and she looks after and nurtures them until they are empowered enough to stand on their own. In the Bardic grade, the focus is on the Goddess, whereas the God is studied in the Ovate grade. In the Druid grade, aspirants learn to embody and channel divinity itself.

The Dark Earth Mother

The Welsh goddess Ceridwen is the Dark Earth Mother. She is also known as the Great White Sow, possibly because this animal is both a good mother and characterizes the Full Moon. Bards are called Ceridwen's piglets, and she loves and protects them fiercely until they are weaned and able to look after themselves. In many cultures, the Goddess is recognized as the Source of true power, the being who gives us the energy to realize our dreams of the Sacred. In India, she has many names, including Shakti and kundalini.

In the Celtic world, the Goddess is known as Ceridwen, Bridget, and the Morrigan, a fierce goddess who looks over the life, death, and fates of humankind. The Morrigan challenges anyone making their bid for spiritual power: How far are you prepared to go? How much are you prepared to sacrifice in order to awaken the spiritually potent archetype that lives within? The Morrigan also embodies the spirit of the land, and whoever decides to awaken their Spiritual Warrior within is required to marry her. This sacred relationship is a full partnership, and it lasts, for better or worse, forever. She responds very positively to commitment.

If you commit yourself to the Druid path, she will fully support your endeavors.

Beware anyone who reneges on his or her vows, however! In the legends, the Morrigan also gets very annoyed if we do not recognize her, or either reject or ignore her. The more successful the relationship between you and the Morrigan, the more empowered you will become. If she feels unconditionally loved and honored, she will bestow the gift of sovereignty on you.

To pursue a fully committed Druidic path, you must awaken and commit yourself to the well-being and health of the Goddess, the sacred Earth, and the spiritually empowered feminine that lives within. The Goddess may manifest as a physical partner, as all women, as power, or as a mixture of all these. She is the spirit of the Earth, our wonderful planet, the Great Goddess who births us and gives us the substance of life itself—our bodies.

Make no mistake; if you make your bid for power, she will be there. If you are ready to surrender to the power that rules your fate and take up the reins of your destiny, you will have great things to offer your community, your land, and your planet. You will be working hand in hand, and heart to heart, with the Great Goddess herself. Indeed, your destiny is to realize that you *are* the Goddess and are at One with her. When you have completed your Earth walk, you will return to her and unite with her for all time.

The Goddess presents a choice to everyone considering dedicating his or her life to Druidry. How far will you attempt to go? Will you devote yourself fully to a life of spiritual development, surrendering your own desires to the will of the Divine? Will you use your growing spiritual power to create a comfortable, well-paid, happy, successful, yet conventional lifestyle? Or will you settle for a compromise somewhere between the two?

Confronted by this dilemma, you soon realize that there is actually no choice. In order to create and live a spontaneous life filled with Spirit (the Awen), you must leave your former life behind and start on a one-way journey that will take you through the unknown on your own unique path, leading to spiritual power and freedom. This path leads to the direct experience of the Sacred.

This doesn't mean you should suddenly leave your home and wife and kids and incarcerate yourself for the rest of your life in a monastery! Unlike many others on spiritual paths, Druids become empowered by full immersion in the world, accepting their physical lives as creations that only come alive when they are fully lived and loved. They also recognize their bodies as temples for their souls, caring for them in order to keep them healthy and happy. They strive to embrace their families, friends, homes, communities, work, and land with love and compassion, which is the way the Sacred manifests on Earth.

The Challenge of the Morrigan

Once upon a time, a long time ago, a young lad named Fionn set out to find his destiny. In that time, the countryside was dark and dangerous. Wild animals lurked in the shadows, the elements were capricious and sometimes fierce, and criminals were always ready to remove valuables from—or even kill—unwary travelers. Worst of all were the strange and frightening magical entities that roamed the land and fed off the energies of anyone unfortunate enough to be caught unawares. At best, these encounters were very unpleasant; at worst, they resulted in shock, insanity, or even death.

Fionn had already made his decision to leave home to find his fame and fortune and had accepted the many possible hardships that might befall him on his journey. At peace with his fate, he walked the countryside, carrying his hurling stick and ball and playing with them as he walked. At night, he slept on a mattress of leaves and moss, with a stone as his pillow and his cloak as a blanket. All was not as it seemed, however. There was magic afoot. Despite his youth and alertness, he was unaware that he was being followed by a shadow—the shadow of a raven who was far enough away to be unobtrusive but close enough to be a constant presence.

On the third morning, when he awoke, Fionn emerged from his sleeping hole by the side of the road to find a woman standing over him. She seemed taller and darker than any adult he had ever seen, but he assumed that was the effect of the light of the Sun, which was rising over the horizon behind her. As his eyes became accustomed to the light, he saw that she had wild red hair and flashing green eyes. Her cloak was dark green with black feathers as highlights that stirred in a breeze he couldn't feel. She wore a golden torc, the sign of a queen, around her neck. In one hand, she carried a spear with a long, razor-sharp blade; in the other, she carried a stout wooden shield inlaid with intricate, metallic knot work. Her sandals were made of leather, fastened with thongs.

The figure had an air of warmth about her, tempered by a sense of absolute authority. You wouldn't want her as an enemy. She was extremely beautiful but had the type of beauty you see in a thunderstorm or in wild tempestuous seas.

"Do not be afraid," she said. "I am a great queen of this island, and I have been watching over you for a long while. I am here to tell you your destiny." She sat down on the ground and faced the boy.

"If you want it, you will have a long and happy life with a good home, a beautiful wife, and children who will love you well. And when you die, you will be old, well-loved, and happy."

The boy thought about this possible future, interested but hesitant.

"But there is another possible life for you," continued the powerful woman. "You can leave your old life and live with me. You can serve me, and I will give you magic and an insatiable capacity for life. You can open yourself to my healing powers and transform yourself into a spiritual warrior of wisdom and power, sharing my dream to heal the land and all that lives upon it. You can live your life to the absolute fullest, becoming a great hero and knowing adventure, passion, and danger. If you choose this life, you will create a great name for yourself. The poets and storytellers will tell your tale forevermore. But you will die young, in your prime."

The woman stood again, and Fionn wondered at her beauty and her mein of absolute authority.

"I offer you a choice today," she said. "The decision you make will transform your future irrevocably. Which life will you choose?"

Without hesitation, Fionn made his decision.

THE WIZARD

Two of the most famous Druids are Merlin and Taliesin, although not much is known about either as historical figures. Merlin is a powerful wizard who devotes his life to manifesting the Sacred on Earth. He is the servant of King Arthur and the sacred land of Albion, the oldest known name for Britain. Taliesin is a bard, using the power of words to bring the Sacred to Earth. Merlin and Taliesin whisper to us through the mists of time, hinting and suggesting who and what they were, challenging modern-day bards to rediscover them inside their own hearts and minds. Druidry is a melding of the physical and magical worlds. Whenever Druidry is involved, there will be few verifiable facts; we are challenged to trust and believe our hearts, rather than rely on dry, logical academic "proof."

What we do know is that both Merlin and Taliesin were poets, musicians, wise people, advisors to nobility, magic-makers, healers, oracles, and historians. They were master wordsmiths, specialists in using the power of words. Allied with music and skillful timing, they transported their audiences into a liminal world of archetypes and healing. It is said that anyone exposed to these empowered bardic skills is changed forever, and that a little of the magic experienced remains forever. The bardic arts were the tools of these two consummate healers, whose intent was to find the lost parts of their audiences' souls and restore them to wholeness.

Arthur and Merlin

Because of his connection to King Arthur, Merlin may be the most famous of the ancient bards. As with other Druid mysteries, there is controversy regarding whether Arthur or Merlin ever actually lived. Were they historical people or merely subjects of legend? That said, tantalizing clues about Merlin can be found in many places in the U.K. Druids say to all scientific skeptics: "Relax and enjoy! The evidence is loud and clear. Merlin existed—and exists still. Indeed, he is even alive and well in this day and age!"

Merlin is an archetype, a magical being who moves through our personal and collective consciousness—sometimes like a subtle, healing breeze, sometimes like a devastating whirlwind. As such, he is immortal and exists everywhere. Merlin regularly turns up in our imaginations, in storytelling, in the movies, on TV, in books and comic strips, and on the radio. He is still very much alive in our minds as a living source of magic, mystery, and inspiration.

At times, when the boundary between mundane life and the magical worlds grows thin, Merlin visits us. His presence is unmistakable. The air crackles, reality transforms and becomes heightened, and we know we are in the presence of the Sacred. The hair rises on the backs of our necks, our scalps tingle, and we feel as if we are being touched by something inexplicable and mysterious. Our perception changes; we start to see things in extraordinary depth. Synchronicities happen all around us. Omens appear.

Although Merlin is specific to the Celtic Mysteries, he exists in every culture throughout the world as the archetypal Magician. He is inseparable from the spirit of the Earth, and works with the king and queen to bring health and abundance to all who live on, in, or above the land, including the land itself. Whenever he appears in our consciousness, something thrills at the core of our being and our souls rejoice. A part of us whispers, awestruck: "It is as I have always hoped and suspected: Magic is *really* real!"

And it is!

I Am Merlin

I am the spirit inside every single thing incarnate in this beautiful world. I am the Sun in its height and the Moon in the night. The planets are my children; they spin and weave the destiny of all things in the infinite spaces above and below. The tides are my moods; they affect all things in their flux and fall. I am the past, the future, and the eternal present. You will find me in the silver vortex of the whirling wind, in the diamond flash of a falling star, in the proud stance of the sturdy stag, in the laughter shared among true friends, in the boughs of the mighty oak, in the sultry caresses of ecstatic lovers, and in the silence of eternity.

The power of the Universe flows through me, yet I am the servant of all. I am the Sacred in all things. I am love; I bestow freedom; I see all things as beautiful. I bring people together in peace; I am the joy that flows to the surface of the truthful mind. I manifest through people who follow the native spiritual traditions of those magical lands collectively called Albion and through the open hearts of all those who can hear my whispering.

Do you seek me? Does your soul thrill when you hear my call? When you find me, will you recognize me? Love and honor me? Will you nurture and care for me and make a home for me inside your most vulnerable center? Do you have the persistence and ability to glean the secrets of my released spirit? Then, finally, when all is said and done, will you rise to my challenge to empower yourself and midwife my magic through your lips, your arms, your body for the health of all beings and the sacredness of the land?

My mission is simple—to manifest the Sacred here and now, in this lifetime, so that the prophesies are fulfilled. I dream a magnificent Dream of all beings celebrating their birthright, all dreams coming true, all hearts beating to a single rhythm—a dream of unity and fulfillment manifesting, and abundance here upon Earth.

The God and the Goddess, the King and the Queen, Heaven and Earth join together in the eternal dance of creation. The clouds and cold clinging mists roll back, revealing the Summerlands, the ever-present paradise that is here for those eyes and hearts that can See. Finally, under the Sun and on our Mother the Earth, we recognize one another as the brothers and sisters we lost so long ago. We embrace, found after being lost for so long, once again in the arms of our family, and we celebrate the perfection in one another.

The Earth, nature, the Goddess in all her moods, is my lover, child, mother, and muse. To her, I have given my heart; as she feels, so do I. Through all her changes, so do I transform; yet, at the same time, I *facilitate her transformation. Joyfully, I make her happy, healthy, and beautiful for the coming of her Lord, the Great Spirit of the Heavens, the Great Stag in the heat of the chase, who unites with her, impregnating her with the joy of the present moment and the seeds of the future.*

The Great Lord of the Heavens is my friend, my teacher, my inspiration, my father, and my child. To him, I have given my empowerment; as he creates and manifests, so do I. Through the inspirations that flow through him, so do I dream the dreams of the future. Like a caring friend, I help him don his fine raiment and escort him to his Love—my Goddess. In their union, I find my joy and become my True Self, the Magical Child, the Wise One, the promise and the hope of all beings.

I am no one person. I am the sacred Hawk of the Spirit of Britain, a title that anyone may wear like a cloak, magnificent and multifeathered. This cloak is a difficult burden to bear, for, in wearing it, I have abandoned myself to eternity; I have become a chosen one whose destiny is to be ripped from home and all that is familiar. But wear it if you can! The Spirit of our blessed land needs sons and daughters to sacrifice their all in service to the sacred dream.

I am the Dream inside all beings, waiting to be dreamed and born into the conscious light of day. I am a magical adventure waiting to be experienced and brought to life. Anyone can adventure with me, for the rules are simple: Recognize me for who I am; trust; invite me into your heart and take the first step! Enter into the unknown with me, and we will journey together along the serendipitous pathway of your unfolding. I will keep you safe and will whisper directions into your inner ears until you find the way home. Suddenly, you will realize that you have become me, sharing my dreams and my destiny, shaping the world in the image of the Sacred, wherever you go.

So when you feel the time is upon you, put aside all meddlesome thoughts and relax into the peace of the gurgling brook, the beauty of the dragonfly with the crackling rainbow wings, the majesty of the hanging stones at sunset. Call my name softly, and I will come. Feel the sensations on your body as I approach, and welcome me into your heart. Whisper the words you need to utter in order to break the bonds of my sleep, my imprisonment in matter, and embrace my delicate spirit with gentleness. Treat me as your inner Magical Child; care for me and love me as I grow and develop through the years.

In time, there will come the glorious realization that I am you, and you are me.

Blessed be!

Chapter 6

MASTERING AWARENESS

Awareness is a precise science that has been studied by wise people over millennia. Mastery of awareness is the art of learning how reality *really* works, and then using this knowledge consciously to create the world that is your heart's desire. In order to do this, you need to know what awareness is and how it works.

Awareness is simply the ability to perceive, to feel, and to be conscious of your life and the Universe that surrounds you. In general, it is the state of being aware. The condition of your awareness depends on the strength and health of your life force and your capacity to live a meaningful life of purpose and impeccability.

Druid awareness, on the other hand, is the knowledge that life is so vast that it is actually an incomprehensible mystery. Druids take on the challenge of increasing their awareness. To succeed in this, they must constantly, consciously interact with the world and explore the mystery. As they gain personal experience of the mystery, they transform the unknown into the known.

The mastery of awareness has many levels. Here, we will start with the first level—bardic awareness. The human condition is such that, under normal conditions, all the life force we are able to access is completely used up in the habitual physical, emotional, and mental activities of our daily lives. There is a reserve of energy that is available to some people in emergencies, but, under normal conditions, our lives settle into the status quo within safe and comfortable boundaries.

If all your personal power is being consumed by your habitual acts, then obviously you must change your life in ways that will consume less energy and generate more if you wish to grow and increase your awareness. This is the Warrior's task, because people who desire normality above all else aren't suddenly going to change and become adventurers of the unknown without good reason! Therefore, the first thing you must do is to access and activate the Warrior that lives dormant within you. Bards do this formally about half way through their training, in a rite of passage that activates their inner Warrior and transforms their familiar lives into a quest for wholeness.

To increase your level of life force, you must understand the principles of awareness, see how they apply to you specifically, and then take appropriate action. This entails getting clear about how you utilize your energies and completely upgrading the way you manage them. First, you must identify the acts and experiences that make you joyful and that generate positive energy. Once you have done this, you can build more of them into your life. Then you must find the habits and practices that make you unhappy and drain you of energy. You can either eradicate these from your life or transform them into positive experiences. The sum total of these changes will result in an excess of energy, which you can then utilize for self-transformation.

In order to change your behavior, you need a strategy. Once you have identified your positive and negative traits, make a list of both. For each item on the list, make a plan. For instance, if you feel good after playing tennis once a week, book a second session. If you feel drained by doing a job you don't like, start looking for a more satisfying type of employment. It's common sense, really, but few people are able to perceive life in such clear ways or are prepared to take remedial action.

Another very effective way to generate excess energy is to start a daily spiritual practice. There are many practices and techniques to choose from. In Druidic training, bards learn breathing techniques that concentrate the mind. Magical and healing work is greatly facilitated by a focused mind. Constant, determined, regular practice generates a powerful momentum, that enables practitioners to access ever-increasing amounts of beneficial energy. Whatever technique you choose as a daily practice, make sure it helps to increase your awareness and enhances your training as a Warrior.

The ability to awaken and stay alert at all times is an essential skill of a Warrior. This is called *situational awareness*, an instinctual state of consciousness inherent in wild animals. Getting in touch with your inner Hunter in its aspect as a power animal is a great way to develop your instinctual awareness. In chapter 8, I give examples of shamanic journeys that can help you identify and interact with your own power animal. Once you have identified this aspect of yourself, you must build a deep and loving relationship with it. You can do this by researching it, interacting with it, merging with it, and integrating its behavior into your life.

PRINCIPLES OF BARDIC AWARENESS

Developing your awareness helps you get clear about your life, aligns you to the Sacred, and enables you to become ever more alive. It is not enough to learn about awareness intellectually, however. In order to make any difference at all, it is essential that you put what you learn into practice and integrate it into your life. Bards learn, first and foremost, that true reality is not "out there" and that life isn't what it seems to be. They come to know that the truth lies within, in the heart. Druids call the physical world the "apparent world" to indicate that it reflects only what reality *appears* to be, not what it truly is.

We have been taught that only what we can see and touch is reality; everything else is either imaginary or nonsense. In order to become a Druid, however, you must understand the true nature of reality. To accomplish this, you must increase your levels of awareness.

There are twelve basic principles of bardic awareness. By studying them and seeing how they relate to your everyday life, you can start to experiment with them and learn how to use them. By putting them into practice and integrating them into your world, you can make huge leaps in awareness.

The first principle states that awareness is a skill that can be learned, practiced, and increased almost infinitely. Awareness is a state that must be encouraged and practiced with great determination if you want to transform your view of the world. Mastery of awareness is accomplished only when its twelve principles have been fully integrated into your everyday life.

The second principle states that we are all beings of light in a Universe consisting of pure energy in constant motion, and this energy is sentient. Your energy body is an egg-shaped aura of light, extending about an arm's length outside your physical form, with its pointed end downward. A healthy aura is an alive, sentient, scintillating, dancing, otherworldly lightshow and is a wonder to behold. Everything in the outer Universe is contained within your energy body, and vice versa. The old saying "As above, so below" is literally correct. In this case, however, perhaps it should be: "As inside, so outside."

The third principle is that your awareness is proportional to your personal power. In other words, the more energy you have, the more aware you are. In order to develop in awareness, you must find ways to increase your levels of life force. You must become a hunter of energy.

The fourth principle is that energy follows thought. That is, the thoughts, beliefs, and attitudes you hold create your reality, and they have immediate consequences. In order to create the reality your soul needs to thrive, you must change the quality and quantity of your thoughts (your internal dialogue) to resonate with the world, or state of consciousness, in which you wish to live. This principle has far-reaching effects.

The fifth principle follows from the fourth. It states that what you perceive outside yourself is a perfect reflection of your inner reality. As above, so below. As outside, so inside. This mirror phenomenon is the best tool you have for discovering who and what you truly are. All you have to do is observe the world around you, see how it affects you—and there you are, in all your glory! By consciously using other people as our mirrors, we learn an enormous amount about ourselves, simply because it is always much easier to see the virtues and vices in other people than it is to see them in ourselves. Also, if we know that the action of another person is merely a reflection of an aspect of ourselves, then no matter how unpleasant the action may be, when we point a finger at that person, we actually point the finger at ourselves.

Know Thyself

The precept "Know Thyself" is at the heart of all Mystery schools. If we truly know ourselves, we know everything, for the Universe exists equally within and outside ourselves. A consequence of this rule is that we can only change the outer world by changing ourselves. Even the most powerful magician or dictator cannot manipulate the "outside" world simply to satisfy his own desires, but he *can* change himself. Mahatma Gandhi once said: "Be the change you want to see in the world." Wise words indeed.

The sixth principle states that the path of the Druid is one of full immersion in life. Your destiny cannot be changed, yet you have the power to choose how to interact with it as it manifests. Therefore, Druids are challenged to enter life fully, with courage and determination, in order to give themselves the opportunity to grow, transform, and come alive to their greatest potential. You cannot deny this one and precious life by living as a recluse or in a monastery. You must embrace it as a lover or a dance partner and engage it with passion and wild abandon!

The seventh principle states that creating your freedom is only possible if you take full responsibility for your life. By blaming or indulging in victim consciousness, you disempower yourself. Being aware that life is an exact mirror of yourself is of no use if you experience it from the viewpoint of a victim. Life is not something that simply happens to you. By taking responsi-

The Bardic Book of Becoming

bility for the fruits of your every thought, word, and deed—past and present—you empower yourself to become an active creator of the truth of the present moment. If you take responsibility for creating your reality, you empower yourself to change it. By changing reality according to your heart's desires, you earn your freedom.

The eighth principle of awareness states that the only goals that have any relevance are the dreams of our hearts; anything else is, ultimately, a waste of time and thus an energy drain. By observing and interacting with the mirror of life, you find out who you are and what you care about. Over time, you rearrange the content of your life, increasing those things that bring you alive and discarding the rest. Your world then grows steadily in aliveness and passion, causing your energy levels to increase. This process is called finding, or creating, your path with heart. When confronted with a decision, ask yourself: "Does this path have heart?" Then listen carefully to how your heart replies and act accordingly.

The ninth principle states that only single-minded, focused effort over a long period of time will generate enough energy to make your dreams come true. Success is *not* related to the result of your struggle but to the impeccability you apply to it. Remember—the whole point of life is to *live* it. So it is the journey that is important! With unswerving perseverance, you will eventually make your dreams come true. Druids develop their spiritual power by manifesting the dreams of their hearts, whatever the cost.

The tenth principle states that any increase in awareness comes from your own personal experience and cannot be gained through proxy. Growth and evolution only happen when you face your life fully and dance with it with all the energy you can muster.

The eleventh principle states that there are only two types of failure: giving up and not starting in the first place. Our parents, teachers, and authority figures teach us that, if we fail repeatedly at something, we may as well give up and try something else. And many people have lofty dreams but don't even try to realize them because it all seems too long a process, or too inconvenient, or too difficult. Where will they end up? Nowhere near the place or state for which their hearts yearn. Druids get clear about where their hearts' longing lies and, even if it seems hopeless, don't stop trying until they manifest it!

The twelfth and final principle states that your awareness is proportional to the extent you live in the present—the "eternal now." Much of the practical healing work students undertake is directed toward recovering energy they have left in the past, and retrieving energy they have projected into the future through fantasies, hopes, and fears. All your projected energies must be brought back into the present so you can become whole again. Few of us actually live in the present. But if you are not present, then where are you? If you are not in the here and now, you are not truly living; you are drifting about in a fantasy while life passes you by. Too soon, you realize that you are old, and it is all too late.

Failing to enjoy the present moment can make you heavy, dull, and boring—signs of low-energy and fragility. When you commit yourself to live fully in the here and now, you become a healthy and happy Magical Child. You find your soul and become a whole being once again. A person who lives completely in the here and now is said to have *presence*. Are you ready to take the challenge?

The Bardic Book of Becoming

A Practical Strategy for Life

Here is a light-hearted take on awareness, given to me by one of my teachers, Ken Eagle Feather, a.k.a. Ken Smith:

- Make a list of worries that you can't do anything about.

- Make a list of worries you can do something about.

- Make a list of all your hopes and dreams of filling your life with beauty.

- Throw away the first list.

- Take action on the second list.

- Develop the third list.

- Do daily spiritual practice to minimize your worries and manifest your dreams.

- Complete your life on Earth as impeccably as you can.

INTUITION

Our elders and betters have told us not to indulge in useless dreaming but to focus in on the physical world, for what is solid is real. But Druids beg to differ with this version of the truth and use the metaphor of an iceberg to shed light on the nature of reality. The ancients knew that the visible—what we can talk about and explore with our logical, rational minds—is only a small fraction of the whole, and that what lies beneath the surface is by far the larger portion of reality. The infinite space that joins these two aspects of reality represents Spirit, which is unfathomable and cannot be thought about or described in words. And this is the Druid's challenge—to explore and bring to consciousness the hidden realm, to make the unknown known, to make the unconscious conscious. Their tool for shining light into these shadowy realities is a sixth sense called *intuition*.

Humans have two types of awareness: rational and irrational. The right side of the brain is the thinking, logical, rational side. Here, all knowledge flows in a linear, sequential mode, and can be symbolized by the visible part of an iceberg. The left side of the brain is the feeling, irrational side, which operates independently of any logical or linear progression or sequential thought patterns. This is your intuitive side and can be represented by the invisible, larger part of an iceberg floating below the surface of the sea.

The way each of us perceives and interprets life is unique. Your unique view of the world is constantly changing, within certain "tolerable" limits, and reflects back to you your understanding of what life is all about, added to what you consider acceptable. If you decide to remain on safe, familiar ground—in the "known," avoiding change—then your perception remains fixed. This causes repetition and habitual behavior. Moreover, the reverse is equally true. Repetition fixes your perception ever more firmly, which gives rise to monotony and boredom.

Conversely, if you dedicate your life to exploring the unknown and bringing it to consciousness, your life constantly becomes richer and more abundant. You open yourself to life in its totality and therefore to risk. You accept the shadows as well as the light. You feel lighter and experience increased freedom, and your life force increases. And your view of the world changes correspondingly. You partake of the adventure of life and become a spontaneous, fluid, magical being. Druids find this the most exciting, empowering, and enjoyable game in town!

Moods are indicators of your level of awareness. They are constantly changing and are, like the tides, ruled by the Moon. As they change, so your perception of the world changes. If your energy levels are high, your mood is relaxed, happy, and centered. If your energy levels are low, your mood is depressed, angry, scattered, or confused. Your view of the world mirrors your internal state. The wise people of the East call this natural, fluid nature of reality the "illusion of life."

It is your challenge—and responsibility—to manage and maintain your awareness at an optimum level. You can do this by remembering *not* to take the evidence of your senses as absolute truth, because your interpretation of life is dependent on your constantly fluctuating energy levels. Instead, use as your yardstick that constant, peaceful, and energetic state you experience in the presence of the Sacred. By remembering, or even evoking, this state of consciousness, even in the midst of raging emotional storms, you can experience life in its beauty and wholeness. This memory, which you can access at any time, resides in your heart.

HARNESSING PERSONAL POWER

The task of Druids is to increase their levels of awareness to that of the Sacred. But to increase your levels of life force, also called *personal power*, you need an excess of energy. Therefore, you need to become a Hunter—a hunter of energy. As a hunter, you must research your prey, observe its habits, and learn how to track and then trap it. In this way, you create the conditions to grow, evolve, and eventually become whole. This hunt is explored in depth in the Ovate grade.

Mastering Awareness

The word "power" has become very politically incorrect. A huge amount of denial has been projected upon it, which makes it seriously misunderstood and abused. Power is actually quite an innocent and versatile word with many meanings and uses. Druids use it most often in the context of *energy*, or the capacity to do something.

Meanings of "Power"

- Capacity to do something

- Strength

- Control and influence

- Political control

- Authority to act

- Someone in control

- An important country

- Persuasiveness

- Skill

- Measure of rate of doing work

- Energy to drive machinery

- Electricity

- Number of multiplication operations

- Magnifying ability

Druids also use this word in a way not found in any dictionary. They use it to describe a force greater than themselves—for instance, a god, a deity, or the Great Spirit. For instance, they may say during a ceremony that "Power has entered the circle." In fact, there is so much intensity and charge contained in this important word that Druids use it often in order to reclaim it and return it to its original meaning. As your relationship is with this word, so it is with your life.

With power, however, comes responsibility. Whenever you become more aware and increase your levels of personal power, the potential to affect and impact your environment increases proportionally. Druids try to walk lightly on the land, creating minimal disturbance in their passing. Consequently, they must become increasingly aware of the potential effects of everything they think, say, and do.

The majority of humans are timid and suppress their energy in order to hide their true radiance. They can sense that life is not all safe and fluffy and imagine all sorts of monsters just out of their line of sight that are out to get them. Instinctively, they keep their heads down to avoid being noticed. Although there is some truth to this view of the world, it is, ultimately, just that—a view of the world. There are other views that offer better and healthier attitudes toward life. Allowing fear to run your life is not a good way to live. If you risk nothing, you gain nothing. If you are inspired to take part in the dance that is life on Earth, you must be aware of the risks involved, and then prepare to meet them. Once you are ready, you must enter the arena with confidence and panache!

During their first year of training, bards are instructed and encouraged to set out on a definitive journey whose goal is to connect with and engage in life in a conscious, magical way. This is an important rite of passage called the magical adventure, and they mark the start of this journey with a ceremony. As the hero or heroine of their own individual spiritual journey, their task is to explore the mystery and go on a quest to find and merge with their souls. A great expansion of awareness often occurs as a by-product of this quest.

Before embarking on their magical adventure, bards prepare meticulously. First, they learn the rules of magical adventures, for how can we engage in a game if we don't know the rules? Then they research the tales of those who have gone before—our spiritual ancestors who have made their own journeys into the unknown. The details of each adventure are highly individual, yet many of the trails followed are common to all.

Next they decide which tools to carry. Common to all bards is their shield. We'll talk more about shields in chapter 12. This magical tool is essential to all travelers on a spiritual quest, and bards create their own shields on many different levels—the physical, the energetic, and the magical. The shield has many uses. It protects aspirants from harm, reminds them of their mission in difficult times, and, through its design and decoration, displays their magical intent to anyone they meet on their way.

Those who dare to increase their awareness become increasingly visible and vulnerable to predators, both seen and unseen. They radiate their increased energy like beacons in the darkness. The greater their power, the stronger the light. Therefore, it is essential that they master the art of camouflage and practice the art of invisibility so that they can survive and prosper in the energetic jungle.

It is actually your self-importance that makes you noticeable. Therefore, in parallel to acquiring power, you must learn humility. As long as you remain alert and aware, and practice

The Bardic Book of Becoming

techniques to dissolve self-importance, concealment happens automatically. Possibly the best antidote to a swollen ego is the realization that all things are equal. Compared to the vastness of the Great Mystery, a beggar is equal to a king, who is equal to a tree or a grain of sand.

On the other hand, if your destiny requires that you battle with a predator, then so be it. This happened to me, and having fought a battle for my life and sanity—and won—I actually gained a huge boost of confidence in my ability to defend myself. No preparation can be made for this type of eventuality; it is an experience that forces you to find your hidden strengths and to use your wits to survive!

Remember: Whoever dares, succeeds!

Chapter 7

RITUAL AND CEREMONY

Ritual and ceremony are an integral part of our daily lives. Although mostly unnoticed and invisible, they permeate our habitual actions, our methods of greeting and interacting with others—in fact, everything we do. Ritual can be found in simple actions like getting out of bed, brushing your teeth, eating breakfast, dressing, driving to work, greeting your colleagues, interacting with your boss, or playing golf after work. As Ross Nichols, the founder of the Order of Bards, Ovates, and Druids, said: "Ritual is Poetry in the World of Acts."

Every culture has its own unique rituals and ceremonies to celebrate its beliefs and traditions. Celebrating Christmas with presents, holly, and mistletoe; marking birthdays with cake and candles; feasting on Thanksgiving with turkey. These are all forms of ritual. They may be acted out unconsciously for the most part. But imagine what power they could have if performed with full awareness!

Meanings of "Ritual"

- The established form for a ceremony; specifically, the order of words prescribed for a religious ceremony

- A ritual observance; specifically, a system of rites

- A ceremonial act or action

- A customarily repeated, often formal act or series of acts

Sacred rites can be performed for many different purposes: to encourage healing, to create abundance, to invite the gods and goddesses to enter and interact with the human world, to celebrate the eternal cycles of nature, to create magical gateways into different realities, to facilitate rites of passage, and to create sacred space for many different purposes.

There is a grey area between the meanings of "ritual" and "ceremony." Although the words are often used interchangeably, there are some subtle differences between them. Usually, a ritual is understood to be a strict, undeviating rite that has been performed in the same way over a long period of time, creating a tradition with a familiarity that unites those who practice it. Ritual preserves tradition, and there are often taboos around changing it.

Ceremony, on the other hand, is a type of magical theater that can be choreographed and performed for a specific, unique event—like an individual Handfasting or marriage ceremony. It allows for creativity and spontaneity. It is often a lot less formal than ritual and can have elements of play and of theater as part of its workings.

Ceremony has been a part of human life since the beginning of time and is inseparable from worship. We have a need as humans to believe in a spiritual power greater than ourselves—to contact, supplicate, and request help from that power. Every religion and belief has its own individual ceremonies, and they are the channels through which their respective gods, goddesses, or divinities manifest on Earth.

Meanings of "Ceremony"

- A formal act or series of acts prescribed by ritual, protocol, or convention—e.g., the marriage ceremony

- A conventional act of politeness or etiquette—the ceremony of introduction

- An action performed only formally with no deep significance

- A routine action performed with elaborate pomp

It is important to be absolutely clear about the intent of both rituals and ceremonies. Usually, this is stated in the initial invocation and steers the forces of creation in a certain direction or toward a specific target. One of the foundational principles of both ritual and ceremony is that whatever is uttered or enacted in sacred space *will come to pass*. This creates a wonderful opportunity to manifest your dreams but also comes with a warning: Be very clear about *what* you want to manifest and *how* you want it to manifest!

Ritual and ceremony create an opportunity for us to contact the Sacred, resulting in empowerment and a real sense of unity for both the individual and the entire community. Ritual satisfies the inner human yearning for contact with the Sacred, providing a sense of belonging and "coming home." Ceremony creates an awareness of infinity and the unknown, bringing us out of ourselves into a reality of magic and mystery. This provides a suitable reality check for us humans, who have a dangerous and unhealthy tendency to think ourselves the wisest and most powerful beings in the Universe.

Ceremonial space is also a magical space of drama, costumes, and the Magical Child, so don't be afraid to come out to play! It must appeal to the inner child, because the true power in our lives, which is accessed through the so-called unconscious, is very childish in nature and needs an exciting, expressive theater to grab its attention. Once the power is present, miracles can occur.

We are beings whose destiny it is to manifest our dreams. Our dreams are the unborn children of our souls that are crying out to manifest onto Earth. And, in fact, all of us have dreams we have been carrying since childhood. Whenever we manifest one, there is huge rejoicing, and we feel more complete, authentic, and alive.

Ceremony is a powerful tool for manifesting our dreams. The process of creation utilizes the same principles and actions as performing a ceremony: getting clear, making a decision, setting intent, and focusing the will with power. Moreover, performing ceremonies also highlights the obstacles we have to overcome inside ourselves in order to become good manifestors. By directing our energies toward manifesting our dreams, all our inner blockages and wounding are brought to the surface where they can be explored and eventually healed.

Working with ceremony develops your psychic and intuitive abilities. By creating sacred space and entering the unknown, you

The Bardic Book of Becoming

begin to explore aspects of yourself that are usually dormant. Thinking is the tool you use in the logical, rational world; feeling and intuition are the tools you need to travel through the worlds of Spirit. These latter attributes are usually atrophied in the average Westerner, yet they are essential if you want to become a balanced and effective human being capable of serving as a bridge between the physical and spiritual worlds.

Ceremony gives you firsthand knowledge of the Sacred and teaches you how to work actively with the Divine. The magical circle you create in your rituals becomes the otherworldly setting in which your inner gods and goddesses come out to play. All ceremony requires is that you "get out of the way and let Spirit through." As is common in the acquisition of any skill, practice and more practice is essential here.

PERFORMING EFFECTIVE CEREMONIES

The effectiveness of a ceremony depends on the awareness present and the power generated by the members of the circle. Another determining factor is the clarity of the intent, usually focused by the chief ceremonialist. This ensures the efficiency of the ceremony and how effectively the power reaches its intended destination.

Preparing for a ceremony is as important as the performance itself. First, the chief ceremonialist must be absolutely clear about the individual's, the group's, or the community's intent and choreograph an appropriate ceremony. The flow of the rite must be meaningful and move through each stage in a clear, easily understood manner. He or she must be aware of all the roles in the ceremony, making sure the appropriate people are chosen and that they know what to do.

All participants must check in with themselves, making sure their emotional and physical states are conducive to taking part in the ceremony. They must be absolutely sure that it feels right and that they are in the right mood *before* the ceremony starts, because it is extremely disruptive to withdraw for any reason after the proceedings have begun.

When participants have checked in with their energetic state and determined that it feels right to proceed, they must prepare themselves. Cleansing and purification are essential parts of getting ready for ceremony, by bathing, rolling naked in the dew (if in the morning), smudging (bathing in the smoke of smoldering healing herbs like sage, cedar, lavender, or sweetgrass), carrying out a cleansing and purifying meditation, or a combination of these options. For instance, I usually take a cold shower before an important ceremony. I find that it prepares me physically, emotionally, and mentally.

All the physical props required by the ceremony must be present and checked for readiness. For instance, are there copies of the ceremony for everyone? If it is to be performed in the dark, are there enough candles in lanterns or head lamps for all the participants? Is there fresh spring water for the chalice? Has the chalice been cleansed? If wine or mead is required, has it been purchased? Are there candles of the right size and color? Are all the colors of the face paints present? Are the brushes clean?

Much of the effectiveness of a ceremony depends on the clarity and focus of those present; therefore, the minds of those participating need to be clear and balanced. All practices and substances that act to distance participants from clarity, or from the Earth, must be strictly avoided. To be blunt: *No alcohol or illegal drugs!*

THE MAGIC CIRCLE

Symbolism is the language of the magical and unconscious mind. Symbols bypass the complications of the logical, rational mind and connect us directly to the powerhouse that lies within, connecting us to the Source. Of all symbols, the oldest is the circle. The circle has no beginning or end and portrays both infinity and unity. It is only the so-called civilized Western mind that sees the circle as zero; the ancients recognized it as *everything*. They called it, and call it still, the Wheel of Life. The circle separates what is inside from what is outside—the sacred from the mundane. The inside of a circle represents something cut off from the whole, something singled out as special, something magical and sacred.

This is why all ritual is performed inside a circle, inside a circular boundary marked out on the ground. This boundary encloses the energies of the ceremony and provides protection against any forces or entities that may attempt to harm or disrupt it. In addition, a magic circle acts a little like a pressure-cooker, amplifying the forces generated inside it. The container also ensures that the prayers and energies present will not drain away, hurting or disrupting what is outside the circle. Instead, they are retained by the circle until consciously sent speeding to their goal(s). For obvious reasons, the participants of a ceremony and their equipment must remain within the boundaries of the circle.

The ancients performed their ceremonies inside stone circles or groves of trees; modern occultists variously use a ring of salt, candles, or crystals, or even a circle painted on the floor. Visualization is also used to create a magic circle, often complementing and reinforcing the more physical arrangement.

All disruptive feelings, either toward others or toward the participants themselves, must be left outside the circle, unless they are to be used consciously in the rite or are to be healed and transformed. In addition, it is important for all present to remember that they are all parts of the Divine, the One. With an awareness that they are integral parts of the God and the Goddess, the Sacred will flow through them into the ceremonial circle, enabling them to change the world.

When people come together in ceremony and ritual, the energy they generate can become much greater than the sum of the separate individuals alone. Rather, they all become part of a greater whole, an integral part of the oneness of life. During a ritual, the sacred circle becomes a microcosm of the Universe. At a fundamental, bodily level, the experience of the Sacred becomes real, and participants learn to make themselves increasingly clear and effective channels through which it can manifest on Earth.

DRUIDIC CEREMONY

Druid ceremonies have three parts: the Opening, a ritual to create sacred space; the ceremony itself; and the Closing, a ritual that releases the energies invoked and returns participants to everyday reality. The opening and closing rituals are always performed in the same way. Simply starting to speak the words puts celebrants in contact with the innumerable others who have uttered similar words in times past.

It is important to use these formulaic opening and closing rituals, for there is no point in performing a ceremony unless it happens within sacred space. And it is vitally important to call back all the strands of your magical work and complete the ritual properly. This is commonsense spiritual hygiene. Most Druid ceremonies are performed outdoors around a central fire. If this is not possible, or the weather is inclement, they can be done indoors by creating a suitable space with a candle.

The ceremony itself can be described as the *magical working*. This can be traditional; it can be written especially for the circumstances; it can be completely spontaneous; or it can be a blend of all of these. Examples of ceremonies are sweat lodges, solar festivals, *eisteddfod* (celebrations of creativity), or rites of passage like marriages or funerals.

By practicing ritual and ceremony, we realize our spiritual role—to become bridges between Heaven and Earth, facilitating the unity of the Sacred and the mundane. The union of these two supposed polar opposites creates happiness, healing, abundance, and fertility. When we create this bridge, we do it for far more than our own benefit. Because our actions affect all beings, the whole world celebrates with us. Ultimately, we help to bring healing and evolution to the Great Goddess who unconditionally feeds, nourishes, and cares for us, her children. What a joy! What an honor!

Opening a Ceremony

The opening ritual is used to create the appropriate sacred space for the ceremony. Only when this sacred space has been created can the ceremony itself begin.

It is important to prepare for these rituals properly. The Chief Druid allots roles in the ceremony and helps participants assemble their costumes and props. He or she makes sure participants know their words and coaches them or produces "crib sheets" to be read during the ceremony. If the ceremony is to take place in the dark, then each participant needs a candle or flashlight in order to illuminate the words. If rain is forecast, those with written instructions need a transparent plastic sleeve to protect the paper. All of these considerations need to be thought through and planned for. Many a ceremony has faltered because the words couldn't be read in the darkness, or the paper had dissolved in an unexpected rain shower.

Bardic Opening Ritual

Bardic opening rituals consist of the following parts:

1. Choosing roles and donning costumes

2. Energetic preparation and grounding

3. Casting the circle

4. Entering the circle together, mentally prepared and already in sacred space

5. Finding the proper positions in the circle

6. Coming together and holding hands

7. Making an invocation to the appropriate powers

8. Stating the intent of the ceremony

9. Toning Awen

10. Reciting the Druids' affirmation

11. Inviting Peace into the circle

12. Inviting the Four Directions into the circle

13. Blessing the circle with the elements

14. Declaring the space ready for the ceremony

One of the Chief Druid's duties is to assemble the group, make sure they are prepared, and then to ground them so they are fully present in the moment as they enter the ceremonial space. In other words, participants must generate inner sacred space before they collectively create outer sacred space.

Participants enter the circle in procession in the following order: East, South, West, and North. The others may enter in any order, as long as the Chief Druid enters last. If the Chief Druid is holding the direction East, he or she enters first.

East enters the circle, stops at the East station, and faces outward. He or she salutes the direction East, imagining the rising Sun resting on the horizon. East then turns around and faces the center, grounded and activated. South arrives next at the East station, faces outward, and salutes the East. West and North follow suit. They then walk clockwise around the ritual space, taking up their respective positions. All participants salute the *sunrise*, not the person holding the East position! The other participants then enter the circle, salute the rising Sun, and take up their positions.

It is important for the participants holding the Four Directions to stand in the correct places in the circle. Sometimes these positions are marked, as in some stone circles. If the directions are not marked, everyone should be clear about the positions beforehand.

Many of the different roles in a ceremony have specific places to stand in the circle:

- The element of Earth stands next to North.

- The element of Air stands next to East.

- The element of Fire stands next to South.

- The element of Water stands next to West.

- Peace stands next to West.

- The circle caster (if different from the East) stands next to East.

The Chief Druid traditionally assumes the role of the East. Sometimes, however, there is both a Chief Druid *and* a person representing East. In that case, the East stands in the East, while the Chief Druid stands wherever she or he wishes or fills a gap in the circle.

Participants must stand equidistant from one another around the circumference of the circle. It is important that there be no bunching up. This equal spacing has the same effect as balancing a spinning wheel.

Before the ceremony starts, the Chief Druid must determine if the above positions will work for the planned ceremony. Sometimes, a little adjustment may be necessary—a participant may need to be allocated a different space in order to make it all work—and this must be done *before* the ceremony starts. Whatever happens, and whatever changes are deemed necessary, the Four Directions must remain in their respective positions.

During these rituals, all participants must stand in the same places on the circumference of the circle. By contrast, in the central part of the ceremony, people often come closer and sit in a ring around the central fire. People can sit wherever they wish in this case. When opening the circle, all movement around the circle must be *clockwise*. When closing the circle, all movement must be *counter-clockwise (widdershins)*.

Once everyone is in position, the Chief Druid asks everyone if they are ready to start, then they proceed to create sacred space together. The Chief invites everyone to come closer and hold hands. This is a very magical moment when all the separate parts

The Bardic Book of Becoming

of the circle link up and unite into One. At that moment, Power starts to enter the circle and the Sacred Ones start to take notice.

In this state of heightened awareness, the Chief performs the invocation, inviting the powers or forces that are to guide and preside over the ceremony into the circle. There is no need to command these forces, for they respond to heartfelt, respectful requests. Druids attempt to work *with* the forces of creation, a natural consequence of recognizing our place as equals who are at One with all things. The quality of our energy and our attitudes determines the energetic flow of the ceremony. A gentle loving circle is better and more powerful than the arrogant, forceful, disrespectful space we so often occupy in everyday life.

Next, the Chief Druid states the intent of the ceremony to direct the energies of the magical working toward its goal, like training the site of a rifle or bow onto its intended target. This is very important, because attention and focus are the keys to a successful ceremony.

With hands still joined, the Chief then invites participants to intone "Awen," which is the sound Druids use to invite inspiration and bring the Sacred into their circles. The Awen is produced in the cauldron, or womb, of the Goddess and is said to bring bright blessings to those who open themselves to it. In a Druid group, the Awen is intoned in two different ways: as three distinct tones and in a cascading pattern in which participants intone three Awens in their own time, creating a crescendo of sound in which some amazing harmonies can result.

The Chief Druid now invites all present to recite a prayer that unites all Druids:

We vow by love and peace to stand,
Heart to heart, and hand in hand.

To heal ourselves, and to heal the Earth,
And bring the Sacred into birth.

If most of the participants know this affirmation, they simply recite it together. If it is a public ceremony, or some of those participating don't know the words, the Chief Druid will invite everyone to repeat the affirmation in a call-and-response fashion.

Druids invoke Peace early in the ritual. Whoever chooses to invite it into the circle traditionally stands in the energy of the West and helps to hold it. Peace is traditionally a female energy, so a woman often enacts the role. This is not necessary, however, and either a man or woman may channel Peace. The Chief says:

Let Peace enter this circle, for without Peace can no
    work be.

The person representing Peace steps out of the West, moves clockwise around the circle to the North and faces outward, holds up one or both hands, and says:

May there be Peace in the North.

It is important that those channeling Peace actively feel it and project it into each Direction. At the same time, they open themselves to the energy of Peace, which enters them and comes into the circle. After a suitable pause, they then move around the circle to the East, raise their hand(s), and say:

May there be Peace in the East.

They then do the same for the South and the West, finally returning to their position in the West and turning to face the center of the circle. At this point, everyone says:

May there be Peace throughout the whole world.

The Bardic Book of Becoming

If the participants are inexperienced, the Chief may ask them to repeat the words as call and response.

The Four Directions are then invited into the circle. This is done to orientate the space and to make sure that everyone present knows, literally, where they are in the physical, as well as the magical, space. Throughout the ceremony, as participants journey through the realms of the Sacred, they will remain conscious of where they are, physically and figuratively. Four is the number of foundation and solidity, so by invoking the Four Directions, a solid, earthy foundation is created, upon which the ceremony can proceed.

Starting with East, those representing each Direction turn to face the outside of the circle. Saluting each Direction in turn, they invite them to enter the ceremony. For instance, East says:

> With the blessings of the Hawk of Dawn who flies high
>   in the clear, pure Air,
> I invite into this Circle the Powers of the East.
> Hail and welcome, East!

Everyone then repeats the welcome—except the other three Directions, who focus fully on their own role.

> Hail and welcome, East!

East remains facing outward. After a second's pause, South then faces outward and salutes the South, saying:

> With the blessings of the Great Stag in the heat of the
>   chase, and the Sacred fire at the center of the Sun,
> I invite into this Circle the Powers of the South.
> Hail and welcome, South!

Everyone then repeats the welcome:

Hail and welcome, South!

This is repeated for West and then North. At this point, only the Four Directions are facing outward. All other participants remain facing the center.

Finally, when North has completed its part and everyone has welcomed it, there is a moment's pause, and all Four Directions turn around together to face the center of the circle. After a brief pause, everyone then says:

May the harmony of our lands be complete!

If the participants are inexperienced, the Chief will invoke the words as call and response.

The participants representing the elements enter the circle at the beginning of the ceremony holding their symbolic magical tools. Typical magical tools are:

- Earth—a bowl with earth to dab on people's brows with a blessing

- Air—a feather or fan to waft incense or smudge around the circle

- Fire—a candle in a lantern

- Water—spring or well water in a chalice

If the person representing Air is carrying charcoal upon which to place incense, it is vitally important to ignite the charcoal *just before entering the circle* in procession. It takes charcoal at least ten minutes to light properly, so it must be lit in advance.

When the Chief Druid invites the elements to bless the circle, there are a few things to consider:

- Don't bunch up! Situational awareness is vital. Each element has a tendency to move around the circle at a different speed. So be aware of the speed and position of the other three elements and be sure to remain equidistant from one another.

- Until you are experienced, don't catch other people's eyes. It is easy to lose your center and get distracted. Focus on doing your job impeccably.

- When you have blessed the circle with the element you are holding, walk *clockwise* to the altar and place your element onto it.

- Do not attempt to "bless" the other three people channeling their own specific elements. Stay pure and focused on the element that is your responsibility.

Now the Chief Druid casts the circle with a wand, staff, something pointed, or sometimes even his or her finger. Sometimes, someone other than the Chief may cast the circle. Whoever does this leaves their position in the circle, turns around, and walks to the East position. Facing the East, the place of the rising Sun, they point their wand at the sunrise pictured in their imagination, then imagine a spark of bright light—white, golden, or rainbow-colored—leaping from the Sun and entering the tip of their wand, staff, or finger.

The circle caster then walks around the circle, just inside the ring of people, imagining light radiating out from the tip of the wand, starting at the East position and making a wall of light completely around the space until they return again to the East. This imagined wall or curtain of light lingers just outside and surrounding the circle of participants, enclosing the whole space and leaving no gaps. The curtain of light then transforms into a sphere of the same light, enclosing the whole space, above and below, within a membrane of sparkling luminescence.

This is a magical act designed to define a space that is fully conscious, protected, blessed, and ready for the manifestation of the Sacred. It is the last in a series of acts that reinforces the idea of intent, boundary, and protection. Once this sphere of light has been created around, above, and below the ceremonial space, the circle caster says:

The Circle is now cast!

The Chief then says:

I now declare this space ready and prepared for our ceremony of (states the ceremony to be performed).

Any necessary instructions—for instance, "Now please bring your chairs closer to the fire"—can be given at this point.

Closing a Ceremony

Once the central ceremony has been completed, the Chief Druid guides the celebrants in closing down the magical circle. This completes the magical working and returns everyone to everyday reality.

Closure is vitally important. If the ceremony does not reach full closure, those involved will have their awareness split between everyday and magical reality. This can result in them becoming seriously ungrounded, which is asking for trouble. I have often witnessed one or more people (including myself) leaving a ceremony without having fully returned to everyday reality and suffering accidents of varying severity as a direct consequence.

Completion consists of reversing the actions taken to create the sacred space. All roles and elements are addressed—even those not invited, but who may have turned up anyway—and thanked for their presence. They are then allowed to leave, enriched by the experience. Finally, the circle is uncast and all participants process out of the circle, the Chief Druid leaving last.

Bardic Closing Ritual

Bardic closing rituals consist of the following parts:

1. "Now is the time of Recall . . ."

2. Thanking the Directions

3. The Druid Prayer of Peace

4. Thanking the Powers

5. Final Awen

6. Uncasting the circle

7. "It is done. . . . Blessed be!"

8. Leaving the circle in procession

9. Assembling in the preparation place

10. Disbanding, returning to sit around the fire, and tidying up the circle

The closure process begins with the words:

> Now is the time of Recall. Let our hearts retain what the
> ear and eye have gained.

Or:

> Now is the time of Recall. As the fire dies down, let it be
> relit in our hearts.

These words help celebrants to transport their consciousness from the magical working of the ceremony to the awareness needed to complete the ritual. When participants hear this signal, they change internal gears, come back from whatever altered state they have occupied in the central ceremony, and prepare to land their starship back onto solid Earth.

The Four Directions are then thanked, starting with the North and proceeding *widdershins* around the circle—North, West, South, then East. The closing address to each Direction is slightly different. For example, North turns outward and salutes the North:

> With the blessings of the Great Bear in the starry heav-
> ens, and of the fruitful Earth,
> We thank the Powers of the North for your presence in
> our ceremony this evening.
> Hail and Farewell, North!

Everyone except the other three Directions repeats the farewell:

> Hail and Farewell, North!

West then turns outward and salutes the West:

With the blessings of the Salmon of Wisdom, who
   swims in the deep pools of life,
We thank the Powers of the West for your presence in
   our ceremony this evening.
Hail and Farewell, West!

Everyone except the other three Directions repeats the farewell:

Hail and farewell, West!

South and then East follow in the same way. At this point, only
the Four Directions face outward. All other participants remain
facing the center.

Finally, when East has completed its part, there is a moment's
pause, then all four Directions turn counter-clockwise to face the
center. After another pause, everyone says:

May the harmony of our lands be complete!

The Chief then invites all present to recite the Druid Prayer of
Peace together:

Let us now recite the Druid Prayer of Peace.

If this is a public ceremony, or if some of the participants do not
know the prayer well enough, the Chief invokes the prayer as call
and response.

Deep within the still center of my being, may I find
   Peace
Quietly, in the silence of the Grove, may I share Peace.
Gently, in the greater Circle of humankind, may I radi-
   ate Peace.

The Chief then thanks the powers for attending the ceremony and invites everyone to gather closer, hold hands, and intone the Awen—either as three separate Awens or as one long cascading Awen. The Chief says:

Let our Circle now be uncast!

The circle caster (if not the Chief) leaves the circle and walks toward the East to the place where the circle was cast at the start of the ceremony, touches the invisible sunrise with the wand or staff, and walks counter-clockwise around the circle. When uncasting the circle, the tip of the staff or wand acts as an imaginary vacuum cleaner, sucking the light and the bubble of energy back into itself. Then the circle caster, having returned to the East, makes a suitable movement to suck up the last bits of the sphere of energy, above and below, and says:

The Circle is now uncast!

The circle caster walks back to his or her position in the circle and the Chief says:

It is done. Blessed be!

Participants often clap or make a "whoopee" sound to mark the end of a successful ceremony.

It is easy to become unconscious at this point, when your concentration relaxes and you realize that the ceremony is complete. But it is precisely at this time that participants need to keep it all together and remain grounded, for there is still more to do.

Now the Chief says:

Let us now process out of the Circle to where we gathered before the start of our ceremony.

The Bardic Book of Becoming

Leaving chairs and equipment in the circle, everyone processes counter-clockwise out of the circle to the place where they gathered before the ceremony. The Chief is last to leave the circle, thanking it before he or she leaves. Only then is the ceremony truly complete. There is a sudden relaxing of energy, and it is over. Participants can then return to the central fire and tidy up their equipment and belongings, or stay and relax with others around the fire.

Blessed be!

Chapter 8

SPIRITUAL CLEANSING

Energetic or spiritual cleansing is very important before and after participating in a ceremony. Be sure to drink lots of water, and be extra gentle on yourself. Avoid any potential situations of conflict or disharmony, and try to create a safe space over the next couple of days, especially during the first twenty-four hours, when you can often be off-balance. There is nothing negative about this. It is simply an energetic truth and a real possibility that must be recognized, anticipated, and managed.

One way to build spiritual and energetic balance before or after a ceremony is to cleanse and balance your chakras.

THE CHAKRAS

Just as your physical organs service and regulate your corporeal body, so do the chakras balance and regulate your energy body. Humans have seven major chakras, although there are also many other energy centers of different sizes and power that channel energy throughout your aura. Your energy body is a manifestation of Fire, but on a higher energetic level than physical fire. I call it "spirit fire." Just as your physical organs are happy and healthy when they are regularly purified, loved, and exercised, the same is true of your chakras.

The chakras are distributed throughout your body at points where energy accumulates and through which energy passes. The largest and most influential chakras are:

- *The root chakra*: centered at the perineum, the point midway between the genitals and anus. It is bright crimson. Its key words are rootedness, balance, and survival.

- *The sacral chakra*: also called the *hara*, centered just below the navel. It is bright orange and is the center of the will. Its key words are creativity and sexuality.

- *The solar-plexus chakra*: centered at the solar plexus, the area at the bottom of the ribs where your diaphragm is located. It is bright yellow, like a sunflower. Its key words are self-esteem and empowerment.

- *The heart chakra*: centered at the heart. It is bright green—from spring to forest green, depending on your likes and preferences. Its key words are connection, love, and unity.

- *The throat chakra*: centered on the Adam's apple or at the throat. It is a beautiful blue, like the sky on a sunny day. Its key words are communication and manifestation.

- *The brow, or third-eye, chakra*: centered slightly above the line between the eyes, in the brow. It is dark blue or indigo, like the start of night before the last light has faded from the western horizon. Its key words are insight, intent, and knowing.

- *The crown chakra*: centered a few inches above the crown of the head. It is usually regarded as brilliant and transparent, interpenetrated with purple, gold, and pinks. Its key words are spirit and connection to the Source.

As you can see, humans are, in reality, giant rainbows! The colors of the chakras are otherworldly, vibrant, and sentient. In the exercise below, see if you can imagine them as especially brilliant, like a bright rainbow against a dark cloud.

The chakras are connected by an open channel designed to contain and facilitate strong flows of energy. This corresponds, in the physical body, to the spinal column. In the East, it is called *sushumna*, and it connects Heaven with Earth.

Imagine looking at your chakra system from "outside" yourself. Allow the presence of your physical body to fade, until it is almost transparent. In your mind's eye, imagine a vertical tube with seven balls of light spaced along its length. The balls are all the colors of the rainbow—from red to purple and violet. In your imagination, your physical body is now only an impression; you can see that the top chakra hovers a couple of inches above the crown of your head, and the center of your root chakra lies just below your genitals.

Now immerse yourself in your body again. See if you can "feel" the presence of each chakra. You should be able to feel at least a few of them once you begin the exercise that follows.

Cleansing Your Chakras

Make yourself comfortable. You may stand or sit, whatever feels best. Keep your spine straight, but not too rigid. Breathe deeply yet gently from your abdomen. As you breathe in, feel all the energy of the Universe entering your heart, lungs, and energy body. As you breathe out, imagine any tension or stress leaving you through the point where your body is in contact with the Earth.

Start by feeling your energetic roots growing downward until they touch the molten, white-hot center of the Earth. Feel how the energy of the planet responds, rising upward to enter your root chakra. Then allow your attention to move up to the stars above your head. Visualize the subtler star-fire energy descending and touching the top of your head, activating your crown chakra. You are now in contact with the fires of Above and the fires of Below, a human bridge between the two worlds. Remain still for a moment, aware of how it feels to be at the Center. Pause for about twenty seconds.

Breathe *gently* into your root chakra and see if you can feel any sensations there. There should be a definite presence at the base of your body. Can you feel it?

Visualize your root chakra as a crimson-red cube. If that is too difficult, a ball of bright red light will do. As you breathe, imagine your breath cleansing your root chakra, gently clearing away any energetic cobwebs, spiritual dust, or unwanted stagnant energy. It is important to keep your breath gentle yet persistent. Send love to your root chakra and will it to come alive in its beauty and power, renewed, cleansed, and sparkling. Say:

Come alive, root chakra—be cleansed and renewed.

Feel its presence as it responds to your breath and intent. Imagine its light increasing in intensity and the chakra growing a little in size. What sensations does it produce?

Now pause a while. Then imagine the energy of the Earth rising from your root chakra up the sushumna channel to a point just below your navel. Here, it encounters a ball of orange light—your sacral chakra. Breathe gently into it and see if you can feel any sensations there. You should feel a definite presence below the navel; some people feel it at the top of the pubic area. Try to identify the sensations it produces. Imagine your breath cleansing your sacral chakra, gently clearing away any energetic cobwebs, spiritual dust, or unwanted stagnant energy. Imagine its light increasing in intensity and the chakra growing a little in size. It is important to keep your breath gentle yet persistent. Send love to your sacral chakra and invite it to come alive in its beauty and power, renewed, cleansed, and sparkling. Say:

Come alive, sacral chakra—be cleansed and renewed.

Feel its presence as it responds to your breath and intent. How does that feel?

Pause again. Then imagine the energy of the Earth rising from your sacral chakra up the sushumna channel to a point just in front of and at the bottom of your rib cage. Here it encounters a ball of bright yellow light—your solar-plexus chakra. Breathe gently into it and see if you can feel any sensations there. Imagine your breath cleansing your solar-plexus chakra, gently clearing away any energetic cobwebs, spiritual dust, or old stagnant energy. Imagine its light increasing in intensity and the chakra growing a little in size. Remember to keep your breath gentle yet persistent. Send love to your solar-plexus chakra and invite it to come alive in beauty and power, renewed, cleansed, and sparkling. Say:

Come alive, solar-plexus chakra—be cleansed and renewed.

Feel its presence as it responds to your healing intent. How does that feel?

Pause again. Then imagine the energy of the Earth rising from your solar-plexus chakra up the sushumna channel to your heart chakra. Here it encounters a ball of bright green light—your heart chakra. What shade of green is it? Breathe gently into it and see if you can feel any sensations there. Imagine your breath cleansing your heart chakra, gently clearing away any energetic cobwebs, spiritual dust, or old stagnant energy. Imagine its light increasing in intensity and the chakra growing a little in size. Keep your breath gentle yet persistent. Send love to your heart chakra, and invite it to come alive in beauty and power, renewed, cleansed, and sparkling. Say:

> Come alive, dear heart chakra—be cleansed and
> renewed.

Feel its presence as it responds to your energy of healing. How does that feel?

Pause again. Now imagine the energy of the Earth rising from your heart chakra up the sushumna channel to your throat center. Here it encounters a ball of bright blue light—your throat chakra. What shade of blue is it? Breathe gently into it and see if you can feel any sensations there. Imagine your breath cleansing your throat chakra, gently clearing away any energetic cobwebs, spiritual dust, or old stagnant energy. Imagine its light increasing in intensity and the chakra growing a little in size. Keep your breath gentle yet persistent. Send love to your throat chakra and invite it to come alive in beauty and power, renewed, cleansed, and sparkling. Say:

> Come alive, dear throat chakra—be cleansed and
> renewed.

The Bardic Book of Becoming

Feel its presence as it responds to your energy of healing. How does that feel?

Pause again. Then imagine the energy of the Earth rising from your throat chakra up the sushumna channel to your Third Eye. Here it encounters a ball of deep indigo light, dotted with tiny, twinkling rainbow stars—your brow chakra. Breathe gently into it and see if you can feel any sensations there. Imagine your breath cleansing your brow chakra, gently clearing away any energetic cobwebs, spiritual dust, or old stagnant energy. Imagine its light increasing in intensity and the chakra growing a little in size. Keep your breath gentle yet persistent. Send love to your brow chakra and invite it to come alive in beauty and power, renewed, cleansed, and sparkling. Say:

Come alive, dear brow chakra—be cleansed and
renewed.

Feel its presence as it responds to your healing intent. How does this feel?

Pause again. Then imagine the energy of the Earth rising from your brow chakra up the sushumna channel to your crown chakra. Here it encounters a ball of violet light. Breathe gently into it and see if you can feel any sensations there. Imagine your breath cleansing your crown chakra, gently clearing away any energetic cobwebs, spiritual dust, or old stagnant energy. Imagine its light increasing in intensity and the chakra growing a little in size. Keep your breath gentle yet persistent. Send love to your crown chakra and imagine it coming alive in beauty and power, renewed, cleansed, and sparkling. Say:

Come alive, dear crown chakra—be cleansed and
renewed.

Feel its presence as it responds to your healing intent. How does this feel?

Now focus on the Earth energy that is flowing up your spine. Imagine that this Earth energy rises out of your crown vertically for one or two feet, then, like water in a fountain, falls over and starts to descend around your body, following the outside contours of your aura. Imagine that it takes on a silver, watery quality and washes you, cleansing your aura as it descends to the floor. As it flows lower and lower, imagine that it cools and cleanses your entire aura, making it ever clearer and radiating a brilliant, almost otherworldly, spectrum of rainbow colors.

Stay with the fountain imagery for a few minutes or for as long as it feels comfortable. Visualize the liquid silver collecting below you, rising up your spine and out the top of your head, then falling like a fountain downward again. Do this for as long as it feels comfortable. Don't strain yourself in any way. Let the last sweep of your awareness be downward. When you feel complete, stop.

This exercise demands focus and skill. Don't be discouraged if it doesn't flow well at first. It requires practice. It took me a few repetitions before I got it right; but it felt so good that I persisted. If you have the energy and motivation to persist and succeed with this exercise, it will become a powerful tool for spiritual and physical health and for increasing your overall energy levels.

When you have completed this exercise, lie on the ground or floor for a couple of minutes, interacting with the Earth. Allow your energy body to return gently to balance and normality. When you feel fully grounded, stand up and say: "I am complete!" Then clap your hands together sharply.

The Bardic Book of Becoming

SHAMANIC JOURNEYING

Another important technique for bringing balance, transformation, and wisdom to your spiritual body and life is the ancient art of journeying.

Many traditional cultures around the world work with a shared understanding of multiple worlds and realities that we can visit in order to connect, heal, and learn. Practitioners often work with three levels or worlds, often referred to as Upper, Middle, and Lower. The lower level, or Underworld, is a place of deep, wild wisdom that is often accessed through a portal that takes you deep downward into the Earth. It is the place of the spirit animals, the ancestors, and the faery races.

When you journey, you travel in your dream body and your imagination to this world where spirits, guardians, totem animals, or other spiritual entities commune with you and help you bring yourself into better balance and spiritual health. These journeys are a type of inner meditation in which you travel into an alternate reality, using your imagination, to a place of knowledge and power. This inner reality enables magic and mystery to manifest in ways that your normal reality prohibits. In fact, journeying is a powerful skill for seekers and spiritual travelers of all kinds to develop.

Shamanic journeying is an activity for the Magical Child—the youthful, optimistic Hero on a magical adventure through life. The judgmental, heavy adult self recedes from consciousness for the duration of the journey. Journeying is simply an exercise to develop the muscles of your inner imagination and give them free rein. Relax! Enjoy! Explore! Release your imagination from the prison of expectations and disempowerment. Allow it to play and enjoy the richness and creativity it generates.

Since this is a practice better experienced than described, I will share with you my own first shamanic journey.

I had registered for a shamanic healing workshop and somehow felt as if it could be a pivotal point in my life. I had avoided this type of workshop since I'd first heard about them, because I didn't want to risk the possible consequences of success or failure—until now.

On the day of the workshop, the flowers were out, the Sun was shining, and the birds were singing. As I entered the classroom, I encountered a dynamic crowd moving through the space, dressed in cheerful, multicolored clothes, their faces animated by the hidden forces rising within. Leo, our guide into the Underworld, was a white-haired man in his late fifties who looked happy and energetic. He seemed relaxed and confident and put us all at ease. At least, I felt as relaxed as I was ever going to be in the circumstances. When it was time to start, we introduced ourselves, and Leo explained that we were about to undertake a shamanic journey to identify and claim our power animals.

My rational mind had already judged and decided upon the outcome of the workshop: these sorts of things never worked for me. In fact, I expected to make a fool of myself once again. But at the same time, another side of me—my rebellious, youthful, vigorous, and optimistic side—arose to tell me that I was ready! I was capable! I was invincible!

The explanations were short and swift. We were instructed to beware of the time- and energy-wasting game of "Is this real, or is it just my imagination?" It is *all* imagination, Leo told us, and the sooner we understood this, the better off we would be. In fact, the entire experience of our lives can be understood as "mere" imagination, he claimed, for we humans have an extraordinary power to project our inner reality onto the blank screen of our surroundings. We "imagine" our entire lives!

When it was time to begin, we were told to sit or lie comfortably on the floor and breathe deeply. Leo started to drum a repetitive rhythm on his medicine drum. I found the effect soothing, and I became aware that there seemed to be some extra energy available to me. Leo told us to state—clearly and out loud—the intent of our journey, which was to seek our power animals and invite them back into our everyday lives. I share my journey here to inspire you!

White Stag

We are guided to go, in our imaginations, to a beautiful place we know in nature. There we are told to search for a hole or gateway that will lead into the Underworld, the magical place where the power animals live—a rabbit hole, a hollow tree, a spring or well, a cave, or even a mechanical elevator! In the world of imagination, everything is possible.

I notice that I am completely relaxed. I wonder why. Tuning in, I realize I am in my child self, playing in an innocent, simple way. I am not agonizing over whether I will be successful or not. It is fun! There is something about my mood, Leo's energy, the state of the group, and the positions of the stars that have all combined and conspired to make this happen today. Leo says it is much easier to journey when your face muscles are relaxed, so I experiment, and he's right!

I enter a hollow tree and find a vertical tunnel. I let go of my rational fears and understand that I am in my dream body, or energetic body, and won't get hurt as I would if I were in my physical body. I trust and drop into the hole. I slide effortlessly down inside a smooth earthen tube, spinning and whooshing lower and lower, until I spill in a very undignified fashion onto a dirt floor, arms and legs akimbo. I pull myself

together, noticing in passing that I am not hurt. I take stock of my sur-
roundings.

I find myself in a fairly wide cave, possibly twenty feet long. It feels
welcoming and safe. Its entrance is a blinding circle of sunlight, and,
from my vantage point, I cannot see much because of the glare.

I move to the entrance and look out. A delightful, emerald green
landscape appears, with rolling hills, swaying trees, and thick under-
growth. Large rocks are scattered about, and it all feels very alive. I can
feel the presence of many animals and sentient beings hidden in the
landscape. It is unnerving, until I realize that my cave is a safe place in
this new world and nothing outside can force its way inside to harm me.
I simply know this to be true, so I relax. More curious now, I look more
closely into the green environment.

I find myself, surprisingly, in a calm and receptive frame of mind.
Leo tells us our power animals are somewhere close; we will recognize
them when they reveal themselves to us three times. I am alert. A defeat-
ist thought wanders through my mind: "No animal will ever appear
for me." I reject the thought and return to my alert self. I wonder what
animal will appear for me. Will it be a powerful creature so loved by
shamanic types—a lion, an eagle, a wolf, a bear? Or, knowing my luck,
will it be a mouse, or a skunk, or a worm? I swallow nervously.

Suddenly, a magnificent white stag appears from behind a tree and
then gets swallowed by the greenery. I am spellbound. I wonder.

It appears again, keeps walking, and disappears again.

The third time it appears, it stops and stands motionless in front of
me. We look at one another for an eternal moment. It is a creature out of
a fairy tale; its color is an unblemished white. And it carries a full and
distinguished rack of antlers. I know what I have to do, and my body
moves without thinking. I walk out of the cave and across the open,
grassy ground until I reach the trees.

There I approach the stag. I am aware of its power and wildness, and the effort it is making to wait for me, leaving itself exposed and vulnerable. I feel an unaccustomed confidence and simply walk up to it. Its head is level with my heart. I put my arms around its neck and hold it close. I feel its warmth and vitality, and am aware of the tremors that shake its entire body from time to time. I feel that we have found each other after a long separation, and that we have a lot to do together in this lifetime.

I ask it if it is my power animal. It doesn't answer me using words, yet I hear its reply. My heart melts! What a magical, beautiful, powerful being! And it is going to be with me throughout my life—part of me, guiding me, protecting me, showing me the secrets of the magical worlds. I ask it if it will return with me to Middle Earth, the world of humans, and be with me in my everyday life. Again, I feel rather than hear its affirmative reply.

I return to myself and walk with my new friend back to the cave. We enter, and then I don't know what to do. How do I climb back up the tunnel to the surface, together with White Stag? For a short while, I feel lost and confused, and I realize I have slipped back into my logical, adult mind. I make a conscious effort to get out of my own way and return to the present moment. Soon, a relaxed mood comes over me. I simply walk toward the rear of the cave and trust. There is a whirl, then a swirl, and then White Stag and I are walking out of the hollow oak tree into Middle Earth. I am relieved, and realize I am getting to know some of the principles of journeying and the properties of my dream body.

The rhythm of the drumming speeds up, and I feel a compulsion to return to my body. I become aware of myself, sitting in the classroom. Somewhere along the way, White Stag disappears, but I feel him close, and I don't worry. I feel triumphant and almost unbelieving. I have done it! I have entered the Underworld and have both recognized and merged with my power animal!

White Stag became my teacher and guide in my subsequent magical unfolding. He taught me how to travel the inner realms, how to access my unique magical personality and powers, and led me toward becoming my true self. He revealed his own unique magical powers and skills to me, which merged with mine so I could develop an awesome way of experiencing and working with the world.

White Stag taught me a magical way of walking that enables me to enter alternative realities in order to interact with other worlds. He has also guided my steps in finding lost parts of my soul, resulting in my transformation into an authentic human being. His instructions have been transmitted in fits and starts over a period of years, and we journey together still. My deepest wish is that everyone exploring their inner worlds finds their power animal, gaining a trusted and loving guide and companion through life.

Thank you, Leo. Thank you, White Stag. Thank you, healing. Thank you, life!

MEETING YOUR TOTEM ANIMAL

After my journey to meet White Stag, I didn't quite know what the experience actually meant or what the ramifications of it would be. But I did understand the main principles of journeying: to state your intent and simply allow it to happen in its own way, without thinking or worrying about it. Simple! You can use these guidelines to meet your own power animal. Read the following instructions several times until you are familiar with the basic sequence, then go on a journey for yourself.

Go to the physical space in which you usually meditate or perform rituals, making sure you won't be disturbed for at least thirty minutes. Sit or lie down and spend a few minutes physically relaxing. Take some gentle yet deep breaths. As you breathe in, imagine all the forces of the Universe filling you, lending you their energy as you prepare to journey. As you breathe out, let any tensions or stress flow downward into the Earth, where they will be transmuted into delicious compost. Relax your thoughts, clearing your mind of distractions and any uncontrolled chatter.

When you are ready, get clear about the intent of your journey—to enter your sacred grove and meet your totem animal. State your intent clearly and aloud, then pause for a few seconds. Now you may start your journey.

In whatever way feels right to you, go to your sacred grove. Greet the space and the entities that live there, enjoying the feelings of high energy, renewal, and peace you experience there. Bask in the healing and love that floats tangibly through the space; here is where your soul can be fully itself and fly free. Stand or sit at the center of your sacred grove in appreciative silence for a short time.

Now, contemplate these three types of relationships you have with animals:

- Animals you have a deep relationship with at present

- Animals that have physically appeared in your life in notable ways

- Animals you have never physically met but that fascinate you

Spend a few minutes reflecting on these three types of relationships.

Now, let go of any stress or tension you may feel and allow it to fall into the ground. Try to find a carefree, relaxed state.

Become your child self, playing in an innocent, simple way. Commit to making this journey fun! Check out the muscles in your face. If you find any tension there, allow your jaw to drop open a little and consciously relax the muscles.

Now, *in your imagination*, stand up. Wander through your sacred grove and find a hole, a gateway, or a path that will lead you down into the Underworld, the magical place where the power animals live. After a few seconds, you will find your gateway. What does it look like? Once you have found it, trust and descend. Then pause for a few seconds.

When you are ready, position yourself so that you can clearly observe the landscape there. Tune in to the nature that surrounds you. Do you see any animals, birds, fish, or insects? You are looking for an animal, large or small, that appears three times. If such a being appears, approach it and ask it if you can touch it; if it is large, put your arm around its neck.

While you are waiting, cultivate a calm and receptive frame of mind. Remain alert and don't be distracted by thoughts, positive or negative, or by irrelevant fantasies. Be patient for as long as this takes.

When you have seen an animal who appears three times, greet it, then pause. Now ask it if it is your totem animal. It may or may not answer using words, but you will hear and understand its reply. If it says yes, or if you can feel it is true, celebrate this magical, beautiful, powerful being! It will accompany you throughout your life as a special part of you, protecting you, loving you, and guiding you through the magical worlds.

Interact with your totem animal for several seconds, then ask it if it will return with you to Middle Earth, the world of humans, and be present in your everyday life. If it agrees, invite it to live in your heart, or in your sacred grove—whatever feels right. Again, feel rather than hear its reply.

If your totem animal wishes to return with you, walk together to the portal through which you entered the Underworld. Trust, pass through the portal, and return to your sacred grove. Wander back to the center. Welcome your totem animal into its new home and interact with it in whatever way feels right.

After a short time, ground yourself in your sacred grove and align again with the beautiful space. Take a few moments to relax and enjoy your sacred space, say farewell to your totem animal and to your sacred grove. Return to your body and feel your skin surround you. After a few seconds, wiggle your fingers and then your toes. When you are ready, open your eyes.

Write in your journal whatever you feel you should record, and then ground your journey further by drawing something that encapsulates your experience. When you are ready, clap your hands sharply and say: "I am complete!"

The Plains Indians of North America have a wonderful medicine story that highlights the power of the vision quest and its ability to facilitate spiritual health and growth. I share it with you here.

Jumping Mouse

Once upon a time, there was a mouse who kept hearing a roaring in his ears. He couldn't figure out what it was. All the time, everywhere he went, no matter what he was doing, he heard this roaring and wondered what it was. Sometimes he asked the other mice, but they told him that they didn't hear anything. No matter what he did, the little mouse couldn't get the roaring out of his ears, and, finally, he resolved that he would try to find out what it was.

Very timidly, the mouse began to explore around the roots of trees and bushes, to the very edge of where the mice lived. There, he met a raccoon, who greeted him. The mouse returned the greeting and said: "You know, I hear this roaring in my ears all the time, and I wonder what it is."

Raccoon said: "Oh, that's easy. That's the great river. I go there every day to wash my food."

Little Mouse was excited, because this was the first time anyone had ever said that what he heard was real. So he asked Raccoon to take him to the river.

When they got to the edge of the great river, Little Mouse saw a fantastic expanse of water. Raccoon led him down to the water's edge. Little Mouse looked into the water, then put his paw in and felt the cool, wet sensation. He tasted the water, and it was good. Finally, Raccoon said: "I have to go find food and wash it in the river. But first, I'll take you to a friend of mine." So Raccoon took Little Mouse to meet Frog.

Frog was sitting on the edge of the river, half in and half out of the water. Little Mouse greeted him, and Frog replied: "Hello, brother." They talked for a while. Frog told Little Mouse all about his life, and Little Mouse told him about the roaring in his ears. "Do you want a cure?" Frog asked. Little Mouse excitedly said yes.

Frog told Little Mouse to crouch down as low as he could and then jump up as high as he could jump. Little Mouse got down as low as he could and then jumped up as high as a mouse could jump. When he jumped up, he saw the sacred mountains for a fleeting moment. Then he fell back down and into the water.

Little Mouse scurried out of the water, hopping mad. "You tricked me," he said to Frog. "I found no medicine, and I fell in the water."

Frog answered: "Yes, you fell in the water. But what did you see when you jumped up?"

"I saw the sacred mountains," Little Mouse replied.

"Now you have a new name," said Frog. "You are Jumping Mouse."

Jumping Mouse thanked Frog and told him he wanted to return home and tell the other mice about the sacred mountains. Frog replied that he could find his way home by keeping the sound of the river behind him. "The roaring that you have always heard is now your medicine," said Frog. "You know what it is and it can lead you home." Jumping Mouse had always heard the roaring, but now he could navigate by it. The roar was now his medicine.

Guided by his medicine, Jumping Mouse returned home and told the other mice about his journey. "I have learned about the roaring in my ears," he told them. "It was the great river. Raccoon took me there and Frog gave me a medicine. I jumped up, and I saw the sacred mountains." The other mice looked at him suspiciously and thought he must be crazy. They didn't even hear what he said about the sacred mountains.

Poor Jumping Mouse was crestfallen. He had wanted to share his vision of the sacred mountains with his brother mice, but they could not see through his eyes. He stayed with them for a while because they were his people. But, finally, he resolved that he would go on a quest to find the sacred mountains. His brother mice warned of the dangers of the prairie and of the eagles who flew there hunting for mice to eat. Jumping Mouse listened, and was afraid.

Despite his fears, Jumping Mouse left on his quest. Out onto the prairie he went, his whiskers trying to sense danger, until he came upon a circle of sweet sage in which he could find shelter from hunting eagles. There in the sweet sage was an old, old mouse. Glad to meet one of his own kind in this alien place, Jumping Mouse went up to the old mouse and said: "Grandfather, I heard a roaring in my ears, and I have been to the great river."

Grandfather Mouse said: "Yes, I too heard the roaring, and I too have been to the great river." Jumping Mouse was excited, because he had found a mouse who had shared his experience. So they talked about the river and the common things they knew. Then Jumping Mouse told him about seeing the sacred mountains.

Grandfather Mouse was silent for a long time, then finally said: "My grandson, the great river is real, and we have both been there and tasted its water. But the sacred mountains are just a myth. They don't exist." Jumping Mouse was crushed by this. Grandfather Mouse said to him: "Stay with me and grow old with me here. This is a perfect place for mice, and we have both been farther than any other mouse."

Jumping Mouse resolved to continue on his journey, however, and left the old mouse in the sage. He went out onto the prairie and, after a long hot day of travel, came to a stand of chokecherry bushes. Out of breath and thankful for a safe haven from the threat of eagles, he lay there panting. Gradually, he became aware of a loud sighing and turned to see a great animal lying on the ground nearby. Forgetting his fear in his awe of the beast, he approached and said: "Hello, great brother."

"Hello, little brother," the beast replied.

"Who are you?" Jumping Mouse asked.

"I am Buffalo, and I am dying," he answered.

When he heard this, Jumping Mouse was overcome with sadness. "What can I do to make you well?" he asked. "Is there any medicine that will make you well?"

Buffalo replied: "There is only one thing that will make me well— the eye of a mouse. But there is no such thing as a mouse."

Jumping Mouse was terrified by this and shrank back. But he felt a tremendous compassion for Buffalo. "I am so small," he thought, "and Buffalo is so great and so beautiful." Finally, he approached Buffalo again, resolved to speak to his great brother. "There is such a thing as a mouse," he said. "I am a mouse."

"Thank you very much, little brother," Buffalo replied. "I will die happy knowing that there is such a thing as a mouse. But it is too much to ask of you to give me one of your eyes." But Jumping Mouse said:

"No, I am so small, and you are so great that I would like to give you one of my eyes and make you well." As he said it, one of his eyes flew out of his head and Buffalo jumped up, strong and powerful, his hooves pounding the earth and his great head dancing and hooking.

"I know who you are," said Buffalo. "You are Jumping Mouse, and you have been to the great river and jumped up and seen the sacred mountains. You are on your way to them now. I can guide you across the prairie, and I will protect you from eagles. I will take you right to the edge of the sacred mountains. But I can't take you farther than that, because I am a creature of the prairie."

Buffalo took Jumping Mouse to the very edge of the sacred mountains and left him there. As Jumping Mouse looked around, he saw a beautiful wolf sitting on his haunches and looking from one place to another. He greeted the wolf, who returned the greeting but then fell into a vague silence. Remembering what had occurred with Buffalo, and assuming that the wolf was in need of medicine, he resolved to give his other eye to the wolf to make him well.

Jumping Mouse addressed the wolf: "I have medicine that can make you well," he said. "I will give you one of my eyes." Immediately, his remaining eye flew to the wolf, leaving Jumping Mouse blind.

Wolf jumped up and said: "Yes, I know who you are. You are Jumping Mouse. You have been to the great river. Frog has shown you the sacred mountains. Buffalo has brought you to me. And I can guide you to the medicine lake at the top of the sacred mountains."

Wolf placed Jumping Mouse on his back and took him up the mountain, through the pines called the Standing People, and into the open country at the top. There were no trees there, no cover, nowhere for a mouse to find shelter from eagles on the hunt. When they got to the edge of the medicine lake, Wolf said: "We are here." He placed Jumping Mouse down by the lake.

Jumping Mouse put his paw in the water and tasted it. It was good, beautiful. Then Wolf described what he could see in the medicine lake. "In the medicine lake are reflected all the lodges of the people. The whole world is reflected there. The medicine lake is the reflection and the symbol of the reflection." Then Wolf left him to travel to other parts of the world.

Jumping Mouse feared being left alone in this open place, blind and without shelter from eagles. Then he heard the rush of wind and wings, and felt a fantastic shock, and everything went still—deathly still.

The next thing Jumping Mouse knew, he could see colors. He could see colors! He was amazed, astounded. He didn't know whether he was dreaming or not, but he knew he was alive and he could see. Then he saw a blur, something green and white moving his way. And from the colors came a voice: "You want a medicine?"

Jumping Mouse replied: "Yes, I'd like a medicine."

And the voice said: "Just get down as far as you can and jump up as high as you can jump."

So Jumping Mouse got down as low as he could and jumped up as high as he could jump. As he did, the wind caught him and swirled him up and up and up into the air. And the voice called out to him from below: "Grab hold of the wind!" So Jumping Mouse reached out and grabbed hold of the wind as hard as he could, and the wind took him higher and higher until everything began to get clearer and clearer.

Everything became crystal clear, and Jumping Mouse could see all the great beings of the prairie—the buffalo and the wolf on the mountain. And he looked down into the medicine lake, and he saw all the lodges of the people reflected. And on the edge of the medicine lake, he saw his friend Frog. He called down to him: "Hello, brother Frog!"

And Frog called back: "Hello, brother Eagle!"

The Bardic Book of Becoming

Chapter 9

SACRED CREATIVITY

Yesterday, a friend asked me why Druids consider poetry so special. I thought: "Why is she asking me that? It's obvious, isn't it?" I mumbled something like: "Well, it is creative expression!" and realized, when I saw the blank look on her face, that she didn't understand. For Druids, creativity is sacred.

Then I put myself into her shoes, and the world righted itself. I realized that, without a Druid's perspective, poems were just poems, the outpouring of a person's creativity, but—so what? I tried to assemble my thoughts and put into words what is simply a way of life for me.

To Druids, *everything* is sacred. This includes the whole spectrum of existence, from birth to death, peace to war, day to night. Life itself is a priceless gift bestowed—by the gods and goddesses, by the Great Spirit, or by blind chance, depending on your belief system and terminology. There are some qualities that humans embody, however, that are considered particularly blessed and that attract the Awen, or the attention of the gods and goddesses, in a special and powerful way. These qualities are gratitude, courage, prayer, offering, eloquence—and, above all, creativity.

The spark of creativity smolders in our hearts, the place where we are connected to the Source of all. It is always there waiting to be kindled. Expressing creativity can only happen when our hearts are open. Therefore, all poets and writers pray that the Muse, the Awen—inspiration—will bless them, open their hearts, and activate the flow of creativity inside. The Muse *is* the Goddess, the female principle of the Universe, who brews the sacred Awen, or energy, of inspiration in her cauldron, or womb. Those she blesses become channels for her creations.

True creativity is an act of birth in which something is brought into existence that didn't exist before. Isn't that a miracle? We humans are channels for different varieties of birth, from bearing physical children, to composing songs, to writing poetry, to developing concepts, to propounding explanations of the Universe, to discovering medical breakthroughs, to acquiring new states of consciousness, to daring space travel.

We also believe that the act of creativity is the main role of the gods and goddesses. They create the Universe, right? But we also create our realities, our lives, and our truths, since what we perceive on the outside is a perfect mirror of our inner reality. Where we go wrong is in our belief that our "outside" experience is the real, objective reality. This strips us of our divine creative natures and makes us into victims, dependent on what happens to us from outside. Rather than proudly creating our own lives, as the divine beings we truly are, we tend to live in a world of disempowerment and disappointment that seems to exist outside ourselves. What strange choices we humans make!

Druids see divinity creativity in each human being, as do many other cultures around the world. Therefore, to Druids, each act of creativity arises in our divine nature deep within, whether it is a poem, a sculpture, or an original idea. As such, it is sacred.

THE POWER OF THE WORD

Bards are associated with creativity, especially poetry, storytelling, and music. Bards consider creativity to be a magical skill that can be developed without limit. Creativity can open gateways into realms that whisk audiences away on magic carpets to their most cherished dreams and offer transformative experiences to their thirsty senses. Stories related by a skilled bard create alternative realities that envelop the audience and engender in them experiences that transform and heal.

The Druids' unique relationship with creation and the power of the word is understood through getting to know their warrior god Ogma (pronounced Oh-ma), the champion of the Tuatha de Danaan, the gods and goddesses of the ancient Druids. Ogma is old and white-haired, yet he has all the attributes of a warrior god—a lion skin draped over his shoulder, a club in his right hand, a strung bow in his left, and a quiver hanging at his side. Ogma pulls after him a crowd of prisoners who are fastened by the ears with thin chains of gold and amber that actually look more like beautiful necklaces than fetters. The chains are secured through a hole in Ogma's tongue, thus he regards his followers with a smiling countenance. From this flimsy bondage they make no attempt to escape, though escape would be easy. They also make no show of resistance and follow with joy, singing their captor's praises all the while.

This unusual portrayal of a warrior god follows from the fact that the Druids associate wisdom with experience gained through a long life—hence Ogma's white hair. If you consider the relation that exists between tongue and ear, Ogma, who is eloquence personified, draws men along with their ears tied to his tongue. His weapons are his words—swift, keen-pointed, and true-aimed—that can completely transform the souls of his audience. He was also the inventor of the writing known as *Ogham*, a magical script whose letters each symbolize the magical properties of one of the Celt's sacred trees. Ogham is thus called "the language of the trees."

Ogma means "path." Thus Ogma was both leader and guide—a warrior king who watched over his people in times of peace, led them to victory in times of war, and captivated them with his eloquence. Bards open themselves up and invite the Goddess to give birth to her creations through their hearts. At the same time, they petition Ogma to teach them the skills of war and acquaint them with his magical tools—his words. Instead of overcoming his enemies by brute force, Ogma draws them into the magical realms and disarms them through persuasion, the spell of beauty, and the power of ecstasy. He is the archetypal practitioner of the bardic arts and is the most influential role model, along with Taliesin, to have inspired bards through the ages. Another example of this archetype is the Arthur/Merlin partnership.

Take note of these awesome practitioners of the bardic arts and recognize their skills for what they are—a type of magic, learned over years of effort, that can change the world. There are two main components involved in acquiring this expertise: first, constant study and determined practice; and second, creating a deep and loving relationship with the Goddess, who will bless you with the Awen. I wish you great success and joy as you go forth into the world and create your heart's desire!

THE BARDIC ARTS

At the beginning of bardic training, all students are asked to choose a specialty from the following options: storytelling, poetry, voice, dance, or playing a musical instrument. All bards are also encouraged to play a variety of percussion instruments so they can lay down a rhythm for their fellow students in rituals and ceremonies. Throughout their three-year training, bards practice, perform, and develop their bardic specialties and learn how to join in shared creative sessions. Bards who choose storytelling collect stories from external sources or their own writings and perform them in front of other bards. They also sing whenever there are shared singing sessions and join in whenever the group makes music together.

It is simple to sing or recite poetry or make music when studying Druidry with others, as there is always a wonderful community with which to play and practice. Studying solo is a bit more complicated but also possible. There are all sorts of different groups you can join and practice with. I joined a local choir to improve my singing, and I often turn up to learn different aspects of dance at the local dance studio.

I challenge you, dear reader, to do the same. Choose one of these creative expressions and learn one of the bardic arts. Coming together in a group or community to share your creativity is such a wonderful way to open your heart and the hearts of others. Playing music or simply singing when outside in nature is also a wonderful way to "give back" to life.

Please take this suggestion seriously. It is a wonderful, life-changing experience to be able to open up your creative powers—to compose and become a channel for your own inner creative expression. To create music spontaneously with others is perhaps the most ecstatic experience I have had in my life. Most groups of adults and children love to sing together or to share and listen to stories. Take this opportunity to become a channel for creativity, the Awen, and the Sacred.

May the Awen be with you!

THE DANCE OF LIFE

There was a time when I avoided dancing at any cost. It was something I simply didn't do, probably as a reaction to being forced to dance once a semester at boarding school. Ugh! And then, nearly fifteen years after leaving school, my partner at the time dragged me kicking and screaming to a five-day dance workshop led by a remarkable person named Gabrielle Roth. My first impression of her was of a thin, willowy, mysterious woman dressed in a black leotard who possessed an awesome air of authority. When she danced, magic happened. She became a mixture of snake, cat, and bird all merged within a human body, and she filled the space with grace and power.

Gabrielle's dancing seemed effortless yet full of energy. I was spellbound when I watched her, which I did as often as possible— while pretending I wasn't, of course. I was completely inspired by her magic and, although I didn't exactly understand what she was doing or how she was doing it, I wanted to learn how to do it, too. I wanted to dance as she did and access that feral power and presence I found so compelling in her. I found out later that, if I had said to her face that I wanted to dance the way she did, she would have said:, "Okay, then dance like yourself!"

Gabrielle taught me how to dance. Not by teaching me specific dance steps but by creating the conditions in which I had no other alternative but to move my body and express my soul. In her awesome presence, and with her support, I faced my demons and started to come alive after many lonely years of paralyzing self-consciousness and inertia. I heard her message: "We can only start to heal when we have learned to inhabit and move our bodies." I realized I had started, with Gabrielle's help, to heal my life.

I learned that the purpose of ecstatic dance wasn't to create a nicely choreographed set of movements. Or to exercise. Or to go to discos every Friday night after a hard week's work. Or as a social event. Or even to look pretty—definitely not to look pretty! One dancer friend of mine wears a T-shirt with the words "Dance Ugly and Drool!" emblazoned across his chest.

To be perfectly clear: Dance, for me, is the medium through which I heal my life, find my authentic self, and become the divine being I truly am.

Gabrielle taught me that the purpose of dance is to experience ecstasy. I wondered for many years what this word truly meant, and I read and heard many descriptions. When I started to dance, and for many years afterward, the vision of ecstasy was only a dream for me. I wasn't even sure that it was real. I wondered if the word "ecstasy" was simply a poetic description of a particularly good dance experience—a romantic turn of phrase used by people with a flair for the dramatic. Now I know that ecstasy is very real and a state of consciousness you can attain through the medium of dance, *if you are prepared to go all the way.*

Finally, about three years ago, I understood from my own experience what ecstasy really is—the unadulterated joy of experiencing my wholeness and authenticity, of expressing my soul while totally awake and occupying the present moment.

I experience ecstasy as a peak experience that lasts perhaps five or ten minutes, sometimes less, although I can slip in and out of it fairly rapidly over a dance session of a couple of hours.

I am filled with a presence I call Spirit, a force that completely engulfs me with a power far greater than my little ego. In its presence, I feel extreme joy, a burgeoning sense of well-being, and an empowering capacity to express myself in whatever way my heart desires. It is not completely safe, however, for it is much like surfing a large wave. It is an ecstatic experience to be sure, but there is always a risk of losing my balance and tumbling into the sea. And, it must be said, the best, most exhilarating waves are those that break over coral reefs!

In the presence of Spirit, I come alive to my fullest potential. I become a manifestor of magic and miracles. I feel unique and beautiful, an empowered human being. I feel like the God. Or at least, I feel as if my inner divine being has awakened. Life suddenly becomes simple and easy, for I don't have to struggle to do things or to try to be someone or something I'm not. There is no conflict or confusion, and I can shrug off all responsibilities, duties, and concerns from my overburdened shoulders. I have a deep gut feeling that I am fulfilling my purpose here on Earth.

The pursuit of ecstasy is a spiritual path well-trodden by dancers and mystics since the dawn of time. Its traditions and goals are similar to those of Tantra in the East. Ecstasy is the goal of the accomplished shaman. It is the natural consequence of having made the commitment to follow your heart wherever it wants to go, as far as it wants to go, without doubt or resistance. It is what you finally find after exploring the full extent of yourself, from the highest, brightest peaks of experience to the darkest shadowy pits of despair. It is the Hero's journey to seek, find, and return with your soul. It is the alchemist's sacred undertaking to transform the self into the gold of Spirit. It provides no easy or quick fix, for it requires almost superhuman determination, courage, and focus. I am not there yet, but I won't cease until I am—which may be never, because the goal is, in fact, the journey.

The act of dancing is a metaphor for life. I see the dance floor as the arena in which I can choose to become my unique, authentic, and magical self. Through fully expressing my inner truth, I heal, grow, and evolve. My dance becomes a mirror response to the enchantment of the moment. The challenges that appear in my dance are my lessons; conversely, the harmonious flows of the dance are my joys. I do not try to avoid anything that comes my way, for that would be a denial of my destiny. I honor and trust my unique path as it manifests, for it leads me to my wholeness.

When I enter the dance, my intent is simply to dance the present moment. I am never alone, for Great Spirit, my soul, and my beloved teacher Gabrielle are all there as witnesses. Manifesting my intent is a great responsibility, for I affect the entire Universe when I dance. Therefore, I dance as impeccably as I can. I wish to express my feelings, my passion, my authenticity, and my self through my dance. I wish to dance my total self, which includes both my radiant and my shadowy parts. I want to be myself and share my essence with you when you are with me on the dance floor, for it is all I have, all that I am. I want to interact with you, in the most authentic and loving way. I want to create something new, something unique, through my interactions with you. I want to share my joys, and I want to dance through my fears toward you. And I hope you will understand that I am not perfect.

I want to be so totally in the present moment that every movement, every breath, is unique and has never happened before. In this state of consciousness, there is no past and no future, only an unending emergence of pure creativity, an ongoing process of birth emerging from the regions of pure potential into the physical. It is a huge, eternal lovemaking between Spirit and matter, God and Goddess, in the creation of the Universe. The Dance of Life. The Dance of Creation. *Om Namaha Shivai!* This is the art of ecstasy in practice. There is so much joy to be experienced by dancing our never-ending, omni-faceted magical selves into existence!

After many years of exercising trust and faith, the dust has started to settle, and things are beginning to become clear. I understand now that I am a *dancer*, and I experience my entire life as a dance. The great bard Shakespeare once said that life is a stage, and we are all actors upon it. I say that life is a dance floor, and we are all dancers interacting with our destinies and with each other—some consciously, some unconsciously, yet all striving to be the best we can, to be impeccable. What a destiny! What an extraordinary, ecstatic, joyful medium through which to interact on our individual and collective spiritual journeys! For we are *dancers*, on our magical adventures to find and express our authentic selves, giving birth to joy, and claiming our freedom to simply be!

Blessed be!

The Bardic Book of Becoming

Chapter 10

THE POWER OF MANIFESTATION

Druids are manifestors. They dream their dreams and bring them down to Earth. This is one of the most satisfying and empowering acts anyone can experience. Over the three years of Druid training, students regularly practice the art of manifesting. It starts simply in the Bardic grade and, as students enter each successive grade, the practice becomes increasingly energetic. In the Ovate grade, students find, harvest, and decorate a wand. Then they learn how to project their wills through their wands to manifest their heartfelt wishes.

In the Druid grade, students take their wand work to the next level. They manifest through the power of their wills, focused by their wands and in harmony with the cycles of the Moon. The objects of their wishes increase in scope and energy, and they start to acquire some special skills they would not have been able to practice without the training. These skills build on the effort they have made during the preceding grades, so they are strongly advised to take manifestation work seriously in the Bardic grades and to practice regularly.

Bards start to develop their powers of manifestation in a simple way. The following exercises can help you, even if you believe you are already a good manifestor. The type of manifestation described here is not the same as you may already practice, for it will lead you into magical realms that can change your life profoundly.

Every month from now on, on the New Moon, make a list of four things you want to manifest. Even in the Bardic grade, it should require no real effort to complete this task. For example, in the next month, I will:

- Say hello and smile at someone I don't know.

- Read a poem aloud to a flower.

- Watch a movie.

- Send a nice card to someone I know.

The point of starting the manifestation process on the New Moon is that, when you want to live magically, it is always easier and more harmonious to live your life aligned with the natural flows of life. If you have a boat and want to sail the ocean, set sail on the ebb tide, and it will take you effortlessly out to sea. When you want to sail into port, allow the flood tide to carry you to your destination.

The New Moon is the time when we go inward and dream—a time when we get clear about the projects and actions we will pursue in the next "moonth." As the Moon waxes (grows), energies grow, and the most propitious time to manifest your dreams

The Bardic Book of Becoming

is around the Full Moon. Then it is time to enjoy the fruits of your labors until the next New Moon, when the cycle starts again.

I give you an exercise at the end of this chapter that can help you hone your manifestation skills. Many starting this exercise want to manifest exciting, meaningful things. Please do not do this. The object of this exercise is to decide to do something, program your will, and then do it. The nature of the task, or goal, is unimportant. So make the tasks simple and easy. Work with the power of the Moon. Make your list on the New Moon and give yourself a month to accomplish your goal. And don't wait until the end of the month to take action; begin as soon as possible.

Manifestation work is simple. Just choose four easy tasks and do them. Be ruthless; temper your efforts with some joy; accomplish your goals. And have some fun!

CATS

Cats are great friends and hunters. They are an integral part of our lives and give us endless hours of love and pleasure. For those trained in the magical arts, cats are also wonderful helpers and allies.

Cats are important totem animals. They represent an unusual number of magical qualities: self-love, magic and mystery, psychic energy, independence, hunting skills, fertility and sexuality, sensuality, self-pleasure, motherhood, love, longevity, and good luck (nine lives), to name just a few. Their time of power is the night, and their eyes are designed to see in the dark.

Cats are extraordinarily gifted and skilled hunters and are great role models for Druids who are learning the skills of the Hunter in order to acquire excess energy for their self-transformation. Watching the poise, focus, control, and coordination of a cat on the hunt is a wonderful experience and can give you many hints about the right use of energy.

Cats have always been regarded as animals of great magic and mystery. In ancient Egypt, they were elevated to goddess status and were often worshipped, mummified, and buried with elaborate funerary rites. They are extraordinarily psychic and aware of the finer, magical energies. Thus, they make fine familiars for witches and spiritually aware people. There is a wonderful book written by Losbang Rampa, a Tibetan master, called *Living with the Lama*. The book is written by the author but dictated by a cat. A wonderful and refreshing perspective on life!

Cats are drawn to spiritual energies. My own cat, Petie, joins us for most ceremonies and spiritual journeys held at our home. She is a great healer, curling up and purring loudly when anyone needs a little focused healing energy. Cats are "walkers between the worlds." They come and go as they wish, appearing and dissolving during ceremonies at the most synchronistic times. They have extremely independent souls and are sometimes infuriatingly individual and liberated.

Cats remind us that, until we love ourselves, we are incapable of truly loving anyone else. They spend a great proportion of their lives giving themselves pleasure. Whether searching for petting and cuddles, stretching, rolling around in dusty hollows, grooming themselves, sleeping in warm and comfortable places, making themselves clean and beautiful, or eating a delicious mouse, they have no problem asking for or manifesting what gives them the most pleasure. We can learn a lot from cats!

Take time to watch cats about their daily business. Enjoy the grace with which they move in harmonious balance and rela-

The Bardic Book of Becoming

tionship with the Earth. Observe how much energy they spend giving themselves pleasure. Discover how guilt-free, determined, and focused they are in their search for self-gratification. Contemplate the eternal question: What percentage of my life should I devote to sensory pleasure? Hmmm.

Here is a journeying exercise that can help you connect with your inner cat.

Journey to Meet Cat

Go to the physical space in which you usually journey, making sure you won't be disturbed for at least thirty minutes. Sit or lie down and spend a few minutes physically relaxing. Take some gentle yet deep breaths. As you breathe in, imagine all the forces of the Universe filling you, lending you their energy as you prepare to journey. As you breathe out, let any tensions or stress flow downward into the Earth, where they will be transmuted into delicious compost. Relax your thoughts, clearing your mind of distractions and any uncontrolled chatter.

When you are ready, get clear about the intent of your journey—to enter your sacred grove and meet Cat. State your intent clearly, then pause for a few seconds. In whatever way feels right to you, go to your sacred grove, then pause again for several seconds.

Greet the space and the entities that live there, enjoying the feelings of high energy, renewal, and peace that envelop you. Bask in the radiance of healing and love that floats tangibly through the space; here is where your soul can be fully itself and fly free. Stand or sit at the center of your sacred grove in appreciative silence, enjoying the features and beings that dwell there. Now, walk in search of the path that leaves your sacred grove—the path that will lead you toward Cat. Walk along this pathway and take a few seconds to enjoy the beautiful nature on either side of it.

As you walk along the path, you hear a flute playing. As you make your way, it gets louder and louder. It is wistful and very beautiful. Suddenly, the path turns to the right and opens up into a clearing surrounded by happy, mature trees. To the side of the clearing is a faun, a miniature version of the god Pan. He is playing the pipes, producing the happy yet wistful tune. The notes he is playing dance through the clearing; they seem to celebrate nature and life itself. Surrounding the open space you see many happy, healthy trees of all types, whispering together in a rich variety of greens.

Animals wander through the space, completely at peace and unalarmed by your presence. Bees and insects hum through the somnulant summer air, and the Sun's rays make rippling puddles of golden light on the forest floor.

A beautiful cat appears and approaches you. What color is it? How does it look? It comes close and rubs against your legs, purring loudly. Say hello and pet it, if you wish, for a while.

Once Cat knows she has your attention, she leads you down a pathway through the forest. Allow her to guide you through the unfamiliar yet beautiful landscape. Cat looks over her shoulder often, making sure you are following. The path is narrow yet well worn, and you can tell that many animals and people use it frequently.

You come to a pool of still, dark water, and Cat invites you to look into it. As you do, the water starts to swirl, forming a whirlpool at its center. Cat leaps in and you follow, spiraling into the center of the spinning whirlpool. Suddenly, you drop downward and land on soft earth covered by a thick layer of dry leaves. You find yourself on the floor of a large cavern, *under the earth*. You stand up and stretch. You turn around and see an extraordinary sight.

Cat has transformed into the cat goddess, Bast. She has the body of a beautiful, highly energetic, sensual woman, and the head of a cat. Eternity radiates from her eyes, and a star shines from each pupil. She asks you to look at your life. Gently, and with much love, she asks you if you treat yourself with honor and love. Are you independent? Do you follow your own star? Are you aware of what you desire, and do you give it to yourself? Do you love yourself enough to give yourself what you want?

Bast requests that you choose something you have wanted for a long time—something that will give you much pleasure. She instructs you manifest it for yourself. What is it? She asks you to commit to giving it to yourself, and soon. You commit to this, aloud, witnessed by Bast. Interact with Bast for a few moments in whatever way feels right to you.

Now it is time to complete the journey. Follow Bast as she walks up a spiral staircase in the living rock. Everything is shadowy, yet you have no fear. The staircase leads to a cave, and you walk toward the cave entrance. The light is very bright, almost blinding. As your eyes adjust to it, notice that Bast has transformed back into the cat you first met. She wraps herself around your legs, rubbing and purring. Reach down and pet her. You may wish to give her a gift.

Follow Cat as she retraces her steps to the clearing in which the faun is still playing the pipes. Make your farewells to her. When you are ready, walk back through the forest and find your way back to your sacred grove.

Enjoy your sacred grove and recharge your batteries for a few minutes. Appreciate the beauty and the peaceful, blissful energies you feel there. Finally, ground yourself, say farewell, and return to your body.

Wiggle your fingers. Wiggle your toes. When you are ready, open your eyes. Then pick up your journal and write what you want to record. You can ground your journey further by drawing something that encapsulates your experience.

When you are ready, clap your hands sharply and say: "I am complete!"

Blessed be!

Chapter 11

THE FREEDOM OF
TRANSFORMATION

How can we, small individuals born into a huge world, find ourselves and become Heroes—enlightened, empowered beings? How can we make our dreams come true? How can we find our purpose in life? Is it actually possible to change the world and make it a magical, loving, and healthy place?

We have been taught since our first breath to undervalue ourselves and believe ourselves powerless. We have become slaves to our conditioning, both social and spiritual. Druidry offers a way to reverse this process of disempowerment, to undo our conditioning step by step. In order to do this, however, we must set out on a new adventure of magic and empowerment to create and find our freedom. As we free ourselves from the chains and restrictions imposed upon us throughout our lives, we can begin to create the world of our dreams. In doing so, we become examples and role models for others who likewise want to walk the path.

It is actually very simple to regain your freedom, but few people are willing to take the necessary steps. Why? Because change is experienced by most as a very uncomfortable and extremely inconvenient process.

Yet it is much, much more uncomfortable to remain a slave, without hope or dignity, than it is to fight for your freedom. Your very soul is at stake here. Druidry challenges its students to enter the gateway into their own unique magical adventures—to find their souls and become whole beings once again. Don Juan, mentor to Carlos Castaneda, once said: "Creating the right conditions for freedom is like moving into a new house. At first it is very inconvenient, but it is infinitely more roomy!" Students entering on the Druid path are invited to join the countless others who have already made this journey in the past and who send strength and support to those who follow after them.

The problem is that we, as humans, have a fatal flaw. Despite all the evidence available to us, we believe we are eternal and have all the time in the world to bumble our way through life, taking the safe routes and denying any reality that makes us feel uncomfortable. We attempt to find a safe niche that ensures prosperity and security, with a few days each year when we can let our hair down and celebrate our good fortune of being alive. In the process, we avoid and distance ourselves from the visceral realities of life. We live our lives at perhaps 10 percent of our potential. The years fly past and, suddenly, we are old, wondering where life went—and then it is gone.

This modern, sloppy attitude is completely contrary to the intent of Druids, who attempt to increase their awareness and come alive to their full potential. To do this, they train themselves to live *on the edge* at all times—a challenging yet exhilarating practice of surfing the waves of life, mostly in deep water, exploring the unknown, and using their wits to increase their love of life. Their purpose is not to find answers or to attain any goal other than being impeccable for impeccability's sake. They are simply driven by a deep desire to come alive fully, to realize their full potential, to accept their destiny and dance with it as whole-heartedly as possible, all the while enjoying their brief sojourn on this wonderful paradise planet called Earth.

Our elders and betters teach us that all joy, health, and happiness comes from the acquisition of physical things. We are taught to focus our magic toward manifesting prosperity, abundance, a beautiful partner, a satisfying job, love and romance, enlightenment, magical powers, happiness, and physical health.

Druids, on the other hand, say that most of the unhappiness we experience in life is caused by focusing our energies on the wrong things—on physical, or apparent, reality. By focusing on "things," however, we actually *perpetuate* our separateness and alienation. We miss the point of it all.

What we really need to do is *find and connect with our souls.* Once we find and liberate our souls, problems like lack, separation, and bad health simply dissolve like a cold, clammy mist in the rays of the morning Sun. You can accomplish this by accessing your Magical Child and becoming a Spiritual Warrior.

MAGICAL CHILDREN

Magical Children are the active expression of our souls. Your Magical Child is your original nature, observing the world through loving and magical eyes, acting spontaneously and directly, naturally and playfully. Magical Children are still connected to the

Source of all things; they are free beings who act out the dreams of our hearts. They are protected by their natural innocence and trust and are guided by Spirit. They are the expression of a fully opened heart. Unfortunately, you have probably been taught to look down upon your own inner Magical Child as an irresponsible distraction and instructed to focus instead on the "important matters" in life.

Druids strive to activate their Magical Children and integrate them into their lives. They do this by constructing and entering a portal—at the right time and in the right place—that leads into the world of magic and adventure. They prepare themselves as best they can, then enter this gateway consciously, while making a commitment to cross the threshold into a new world on a quest to find their souls.

In order to create the optimum conditions for finding your soul, you must make a decision, here and now, to access the Magical Child inside yourself. One of the qualities of the Magical Child is that it lives a life of innocence and trust. Therefore, make a conscious choice to trust this process, which is already unfolding in front of you like a magic carpet.

To access your Magical Child, you must remain in the here and now. Most of all, you must center your awareness in your heart, remaining open, loving, and vulnerable as you enter this new reality. Ask yourself: Do I take responsibility for the choices I have made in my life that have led me to this place and point in time? Then pause for a few moments to consider the answer.

Believe and trust that you are *on target*, that you have identified the right path. You are in the present moment; stay centered. This present moment is the sum of all of the choices you have made throughout innumerable lifetimes. It is the fruit and consequence of your karma, your individual destiny.

A Magical Child doesn't speculate about the future, worrying whether he or she will be successful or not. A Magical Child doesn't leave the present moment to analyze past actions. A Magical Child lives in the eternal present, joyfully—a spontaneous being at One with the present moment, in a constant dance of creation. You don't have to run away any more! Simply being here is enough. Be One with your heart and love yourself. Dare to be your true Self! Stay present, at your heart—and play!

Accessing Your Magical Child

Give yourself at least an hour in which to be fully present, without being distracted. The place is important, too—perhaps a beautiful place in nature, a place where you feel in contact with your wildness and freedom. Perhaps it has inspiring views and scenery. Switch off your cell phone. Have something with you for making music—a flute, your voice—or be prepared to dance or express yourself in spontaneous ways.

Enjoy the space and the feelings of freedom you experience here. Feel very glad to be alive. Then search your memory for a time when you fully embodied your Magical Child—a time when you felt completely free and capable of doing anything; a time when you felt very beautiful, physically and energetically; a time when you were very happy to be alive and bursting with creative energy. You may have been alone or with others. Perhaps your creativity spilled out of you, filling the space with beauty; perhaps your body started to gyrate in delightful, spontaneous movement; perhaps you felt you could magically manifest anything you wished, or you saw the world in a completely new way.

Remember as many details of this experience as possible, and then enjoy the feelings and sensations you felt then. How did you feel, and where in your body did you feel it? Try to remember as clearly as you can what you experienced then. Now realize that the feelings you felt then were the energy body of your inner Magical Child.

Bathe yourself in the energy of your Magical Child. In your mind's eye, try to imagine how your Magical Child would look if he or she lived independent of your physical body. Try to imagine him or her standing in front of you. Simply enjoy being in each other's presence for a few moments. Observe closely, discovering all sorts of things about your inner Magical Child. Be in your heart, especially when you are looking into each other's eyes. Feast your eyes on this beautiful, magical being. Take a few moments to get to know it.

Now start to play with your Magical Child. In whichever way feels pleasurable and right, interact with it and enjoy it for as long as it feels good. Play together for a moment or so, being creative and magical, doing fun and impossible things. Play! Use your imagination! Enjoy!

Know that you can access the unlimited heart and power of this incredible being simply by filling your aura with its energy. If it will allow, practice merging. Treat this like play and enjoy being at one, then separating, then joining again.

When you are ready, tell your Magical Child that you love playing together, and ask if you may merge and live together. Say that you recognize him or her as a long-lost friend and playmate and that you want to journey together on your magical adventure. If your Child agrees, then merge and celebrate! If not, then ask if he or she will live with you in your heart or sacred grove. Play it by ear.

Whatever happens, give thanks and commit to starting on your magical adventure. And be sure that you take the opportunity to play with your Magical Child more often.

The Bardic Book of Becoming

SPIRITUAL WARRIORS

Spiritual Warriors are adult human beings who have taken full responsibility for themselves and for the consequences of their lives. They are committed to becoming fully alive and to fulfilling their destiny on Earth. They are dedicated to truth and are aware that they are slaves to one extent or another.

Spiritual Warriors are committed to fighting for their freedom and to living their lives according to the dreams of their hearts. They understand that the war they wage is to transform themselves and that every battle successfully fought gives them another key to unlock a door inside themselves.

The responsible adult within you is not a balanced being and is not capable of fully finding freedom. Your inner adult needs to join forces with the free, spontaneous, radiant Magical Child that also lives within you. A realized Spiritual Warrior is a responsible, aware human being who has activated and integrated with the Magical Child within.

This is why Spiritual Warriors are so important as examples and role models for Druids. They play as innocent children, yet they are aware of who and what they are. They know what life is all about and are conscious of their every action. They create balance at the center of their being—their hearts. They are impeccable in their thoughts, words, and deeds. They create the very highest energy outcomes with the resources they have available to them. They do this just because they can—because it is the most fun, meaningful, and satisfying thing they can do with their lives.

Spiritual Warriors are beings at war; their enemies are the internal programming and wounding that keeps us imprisoned and distant from the freedom for which we all yearn. They are engaged in a constant struggle to find and liberate their souls. We are "captured" and enslaved before we are aware enough to realize what is happening and before we have the tools and strength to defend ourselves. Waging war describes our unswerving and unrelenting struggle to say *no* to the cruel and manipulative forces that take away our freedom and that leave us wounded and dependent. As Spiritual Warriors, we refuse to play that game anymore.

Our process of domestication and descent into servitude begins when we are children and helpless to protect ourselves. As we become adults, we find ourselves slaves of a system that attempts to create "responsible and reasonable" citizens who are harmless, passive, and malleable, and who provide the energy that the dominant members of this system crave—mostly money and power. Miguel Ruis describes the predators of this system collectively as "parasites."

Let's be clear about this. We are enslaved before we are able to resist or stand up for ourselves. This weakens us enough so that the "parasites" can feed off us. As adults, we have lost part of our souls, and this makes us vulnerable. We may no longer be weak or helpless, but we still allow our energy to be sucked away by others. But the "devil" can only enter if we invite him in. This book is intended to show you that you don't have to be a victim any longer. There is a way to regain your lost bits and become whole again—by preparing yourself and then embarking on your magical adventure. The path has been available to us for millennia.

THE ENEMY WITHIN

The war we wage for freedom starts by identifying our "enemies," *which all reside inside ourselves.* These include fear, laziness, sloppiness, low self-esteem, damaging habits, lack of self-discipline, gullibility, addiction, inexperience, lack of spontaneity and humor, and our ubiquitous, heavy egos (our exaggerated self-importance). Once we have identified our enemies, we must struggle to neutralize, overcome, or transform them in whatever ways are appropriate.

The collective word for our inner enemies is *unconsciousness*. The opposite of unconsciousness is making conscious, or becoming aware. Knowing the truth, therefore, makes us free. By shining a light on our inner enemies, we can conquer and transform them. No matter if this seems a daunting task; engaging in the struggle for freedom provides the experience and expertise that will transform us all into Spiritual Warriors.

We all perceive life through internal filters that enable us to see what we want or what we expect to see. Druids call this our "view of the world." Everyone has a unique and personal view of the world. Druids struggle to loosen their attachment to their own particular views, eventually letting them go completely in order to perceive the truth, or reality *as it truly is*. Much of Druidic training is focused on the teaching that perception is not fixed but rather is directly proportional to our energy levels. Once that truth has been accepted, students learn to hunt for and acquire as much energy as possible in order to transform their perception.

By remaining constantly alert and increasing your levels of energy, you can create the conditions to bring your fragmented soul back together again. Spiritual Warriors do this by manifesting their heart's desires here on Earth. This is called creating or finding your path with heart, then committing yourself to walking that path. Entering your magical adventure raises your energy levels enough to set this healing process in motion.

COMMITMENT

Commitment is the most powerful magical spell there is. A commitment is a decision to make something happen whatever the circumstances, whatever the cost, without fail. It is the bottom line; the buck stops here. You must be very certain about what you commit to, however, for it is binding and will affect your life from that time on. If you are willing to risk committing yourself to something, then all the forces of the Universe will flow toward you and support you in making it happen.

Be warned, however: Commitments are always tested!

In order to create your freedom, you must commit yourself. Half-hearted promises always leave an escape clause. For instance, in order to stop smoking (I used to smoke fifty rolled cigarettes a day!), I had to commit to *never* taking another puff, *ever*. This I have done, and, since then (1992), I have remained a nonsmoker. Never leave yourself an "out." Escape clauses drain you of your energy, your precious life force. On the other hand, commitments that you make and honor feed your magical will and personal power, producing the same results as a successful hunt!

Magical Children and Spiritual Warriors need solid ground upon which to journey in order to create their freedom. The commitments they make become the foundation upon which they build their empowered, magical lives. Stopping smoking was an important magical act in my life; it gave me a large amount of energy that I can (and still do) direct toward my life of magic and healing. Commitments give you the strength, clarity, courage, and direction you need to manifest your deepest wishes. And make no mistake: *Your commitments are always made to yourself.*

Becoming a Spiritual Warrior is an ongoing process that lasts your entire life and beyond. And *now* is always the best time to start. You must make a commitment to become a Spiritual Warrior, for commitments are the only magical spells that can be relied upon to truly work.

Instead of dipping your toes reluctantly into the flow of life, agonizing over whether you should enter the cool waters or not, Druidry encourages you to leap off the shore, from as high a location as you dare, screaming with abandon as you plummet toward the currents of your destiny. See how big a splash you can make! See if there are any other Magical Children doing the same thing, because it's so much more fun to hurl yourself into life while playing with others!

What sort of life do you want to live? A sedate, boring, repetitive, comfortable life, in which everything is safe and predictable? Or a wild, screaming, exciting, outrageous, creative adventure? Do you prefer to take a risk or to have a safe journey? Will you go on a hunt or watch television? Will you explore new, untamed worlds or choose the local pub filled with alcohol-swilling, lonely, boring old people who are waiting for death to free them?

YOUR HEART

On your journey of transformation, your greatest ally is your heart. Your heart is the great, brave, wise, and loving powerhouse that lives at your center. Throughout your physical existence, it constantly beats, creating the rhythm to which you dance your dance of life.

Your heart generates your empowerment as a magical being, provides you with courage, and connects you to your center. It is your access to the Source and to the sacred place where you recharge your batteries. It is a direct conduit to awareness itself. It is your faithful companion through life, giving you joy, wisdom, and laughter in good times, and trust, lightness of spirit, determination, and the courage to keep moving through the dark times.

Yet we all betray our hearts at one time or another. We criticize ourselves when plans go wrong, when we believe we have made the wrong choices, when we lose our belief in ourselves, when we feel stupid, when we do those things we know will damage us—okay, just *one* more beer/donut. We sometimes don't trust the feelings and guidance our hearts give us. Sometimes we deny our hearts' voice of truth and beauty and choose to follow the "reasonable" course of action our heads suggest. We betray our hearts in so many ways!

It is important to build the right relationship with your heart as you commit to a journey of transformation. In order to rely fully on your heart, you must convince it that you will support and stand by it whatever happens. If your heart knows you will care for it and look out for it, it will never let you down. For this certainty and unshakable trust to be created, you must commit yourself to your heart—and *mean it*. Ultimately, trust is only built over years by correct action—by walking your talk. In order to become a Spiritual Warrior, you must build a new relationship with your heart, one that will never be broken. I invite you to do this, right now.

Journey to the Heart

Go to your sacred grove. Enjoy this blessed place, the beings that live there, and the incredible beauty of the place you have created at your sacred center. It is so magical, healing, and radiant! After

The Bardic Book of Becoming

enjoying yourself for a while, invite your heart into your sacred grove. Imagine your heart approaching and welcome it into your space. Give it a heartfelt hug or whatever makes you feel loved and included.

Your heart is all-knowing, in touch with truth, and connected to the Source of everything. It is your gentle guide through illusion, your connection to the Sacred, your ally through both happy and sad times, and the generator of your inner spirit fire! It is the center of both your physical and spiritual realities. Do you always demonstrate your gratitude and honor it for all it does for you?

Whenever you choose to believe your thoughts rather than your heart in matters that really concern your heart, your heart dies a little. And if you do this often enough, your heart becomes silent and grieves your absence. Many of us have lost contact with our hearts completely, leaving us lonely, afraid, and lost.

This may be how it feels. But, in truth, all is not lost. Now is the time to realize the importance of your heart and to rededicate yourself to it. If you make a clear, honest recommitment to your heart and back this commitment up with action, you will be amazed how quickly, and how completely, you can change the situation and regain your connection to your center.

So confront your heart directly, and, in your own words, promise that you will listen to it and act on its guidance from now on. You are a team, and you need to work as one. Using your imagination, if it feels right, merge with your heart and become One once again.

Be aware that you must now follow up on your commitment. Stay very alert to your heart's whispered guidance from now on, and follow its instructions, becoming, over time, the sacred team you truly are.

When it feels right to you, return to your body, and do what you normally do to return fully from your journey. When you are ready, say: "I am back!" and clap your hands sharply.

Blessed be!

Chapter 12

MAGICAL ADVENTURES

Participating in your own unique magical adventure is your chance to make your *bid for power*. It is your opportunity to break through your limitations and accustomed boundaries into the infinite possibilities of the Universe. If you were to let go of control, what would appear in your life? Who would you meet? What superpowers would emerge from your inner being into the light of day? Without self-imposed limitations, what are you really capable of accomplishing? How would it feel to shrug off your usual fear-based lifestyle? What would you do with true freedom, the freedom that is your birthright?

Creating and then entering a magical adventure is your commitment to live a fully alive, empowered, and impeccable life. And it is the only appropriate response for being gifted your one precious life. What are you going to do with the potential that is waiting to be shaped and brought alive? What are you going to do with the garden that has been entrusted to you as steward?

Never mind about reincarnation. You have to make this present life count as if it were the only one you will ever have in which to realize your hopes, your dreams, your deepest longings. Don't waste your whole life thinking that you have time to do it later, when you are more prepared, or more skilled, or more mature. You are only alive in the *now*. Tomorrow never comes! Now is the only chance you have to align with your destiny, to change yourself and change the world. And time's a'tickin'!

The past has gone, leaving an incomplete, inaccurate memory that is dissolving in the capricious winds of change. The future is a distraction, a phantom, a projection of your hopes and fears that will only lead you astray. The present moment is the beating heart, home of the Divine, the only true place at the center of creation. Take up your new role as a conscious creator. Become a cosmic spider at the center of your own web—and spin for your life!

A Magical Child is a being on a unique, magical adventure— in Jung's terms, an archetype. It is a psychological personality of great power that is both shared by collective humanity and experienced individually. When you awaken and embody your own Magical Child, your magical adventure unfolds in front of you like a magic carpet. To immerse yourself in it, you must interact with your destiny—in other words, with what appears on your path—as well as you can. Every moment is unique and complete. Forget yourself and dance for your life!

There are certain principles that pertain to magical adventures that are very different from the principles that govern our normal lives. Be sure you understand them, for they are essential to your success:

• You are the hero or heroine of your own magical adventure.

- Magical adventures are quests to find your passion, your treasure, your soul, your freedom, and your "happily ever after."

- A magical adventure is not a logical or rational affair. It cannot be planned, although you can prepare for it.

- You cannot deny or change your adventure as it unfurls in front of you, but you *can* respond to it as you feel appropriate.

- Everything you experience on your adventure is necessary and exactly what you need in order to create your own individual healing and freedom.

- You cannot do wrong or fail, as long as you do your best.

- Everything will be fine if you trust fully.

- The only way to fail is to give up or not start in the first place. Never ever *ever* give up, however hopeless the situation may seem in the moment. You may beat a strategic retreat when the odds seem too great, but you must continue once you have rallied your forces.

- Miracles are not only possible but also can be everyday occurrences!

- Your head should always be subservient to your heart. Get to know who the boss really is—and follow your heart.

- Although your adventure may seem like a mad roller-coaster ride, with many reversals of fortune, Magical Children *always* win in the end.

- Your magical adventure is actually a never-ending story. If you ever arrive at your goal, take a short rest—and start again.

- At some time along your path, if you are successful in activating your Magical Child and living your magical adventure, your adventure will merge with your normal, everyday reality and become One. This signifies the point at which you become a Spiritual Warrior.

If you decide to enter your magical adventure, all of these rules will apply—whether you believe them or not! Read, remember, and embody them. For instance, if you experience something difficult on your adventure and judge it to be pointless and a waste of time, you are missing the point and a valuable lesson. Moreover, that "something" will reappear in your life in different guises until you finally confront it! Remember these principles and recognize them whenever they manifest—and they will. Respond to them as a Magical Child and as a Spiritual Warrior. Treat every manifestation of your life equally, with respect, and as an opportunity to be impeccable. Do not revert to your former behavior!

Magical Children are creators. This is our birthright. We create whatever vision we hold in our hearts. A Magical Child is his or her own, living magical wand. With vision, intent, and great determination, with constant effort, the vision *will* manifest.

MAGICAL SHIELDS

Your Magical Child has a valuable magical tool that is essential to the success of your adventure—a shield that will defend you against most of the enemies or obstacles you may meet. This shield is more of an attitude than a physical tool, however. It consists of a simple truth: A Magical Child approaches a magical adventure by being wide awake, alert, respectful, and confident. This is such an important principle that we must define its terms more fully here:

- *Wide awake* is a state of consciousness that manifests when you decide to come alive as fully as you can. When you are wide awake, you make a commitment to be fully awake in the here and now, are prepared to accept the truth of the present moment, and are ready to follow your destiny as it unfolds.

- *Alert* means that you are aware of everything that is happening in your surroundings at any time. Pilots call it *situational awareness*. It is similar to an animal's instinctual consciousness, a developed intuition that enables you to be aware of things even before they happen.

- *Respectful* means that you recognize the value and power of the people, things, places, events, and situations you meet on your adventure, whether they are friendly, neutral, or hostile. Everyone and everything you meet has a purpose, a challenge, a healing, and a reason why they have appeared in your life. They are all teachers. Never dismiss or underestimate anything that appears in your adventure. If you give appropriate respect, you give yourself a good chance of learning from the encounter and surviving! Be warned: You will be tested.

- *Confidence* is an attitude that is vital for you to cultivate on your magical adventure. Possessing confidence means you believe in yourself and have the ability to back yourself up in confusing or intense situations. If you stop believing in yourself, you open yourself up to all sorts of negative influences. If you lack confidence, pretend you have it! Fake it till you make it.

These four essential qualities, when they work together, comprise your magical shield. Practice constantly to develop them on your adventure, for they will become powerful allies and protectors on your journey.

When you set out on your magical adventure, you inform the Universe that you are serious in your desire for self-transformation. You are stating your commitment to become a Hunter—a hunter of energy. Hunting excess energy enables you to heal (become whole) and to create the conditions necessary to advance on the Druid path. The amount of effort you invest in your hunt is directly proportional to the speed and efficiency of your development as a Druid.

You cannot avoid or change your destiny, and it is this destiny that determines the experiences you will have in any one particular lifetime. All that is required of you in the unfolding of your destiny is to surrender to the reality of the moment and respond as impeccably as you can. When you do this, you optimize all your opportunities, gain the most from your experience, and thus acquire the most personal power. It is this intelligent cooperation with the forces of your destiny that is the main secret of awareness.

When you gain knowledge through experience, you have perceived something through that experience of which you were not aware before. Wisdom comes from the fruits gained from personal experience; true knowledge cannot be gained for yourself through the experiences of another.

The Bardic Book of Becoming

The shield of a Warrior is a tool that works on many levels. Its greatest strength is its energetic or magical properties. It works as a symbol of protection and also as a reminder of your own true nature. It is very easy to forget who and what you are when confronted by strong and unknown forces, and a shield, when crafted correctly, gives you the confidence and inner strength to face your destiny—and enjoy yourself!

A shield is a portable altar through which we connect to the Source—to our authenticity, our divinity, and our spiritual warrior nature—indeed, to our hearts. It represents the protection and empowerment experienced when we are firmly rooted, awake, and dancing with the present moment. This is all the protection we truly need, and it is the goal of every bard in training.

A shield is an integral part of a Warrior's equipment. It is the tool by which a Warrior defends himself or herself in battle. The shield blocks and neutralizes assaults from enemies, deflecting spear thrusts and the flights of arrows and other projectiles. A Warrior's offensive weapons are the sword or spear—possibly a staff or wand—which are used from the safety of the space that is created by the skilled use of the shield. Any warrior's success in battle depends on the coordinated use of both offensive and defensive weapons and a good understanding of how to use them in a tactical sense. More than simply a defensive tool, the shield is a weapon in its own right and is the definitive symbol of the warrior caste in many cultures. The shield marched hand in hand with the sword in terms of prestige and importance. In fact, in many cultures, the shield was the mark of a warrior, even more so than the sword or spear.

In ancient days, the symbol or emblem of a warrior was painted on his shield. This had the effect of introducing him as he traveled unknown lands. It served as his personal mandala that made him feel comfortable and in harmony with all things. It was his reminder to himself about his goals and a statement of intent to his allies and helpers on the path. It was placed outside his tent when in camp or on campaign, so that others knew who and where he was. The shields of Arthur's knights were hung over their seats as they sat in office around the Round Table.

In the context of Druidry, the shield of the Spiritual Warrior represents the attitudes and inner strengths that you choose to develop in order to face and overcome your enemies. Your true shield is a positive attitude and a strong belief in yourself that will serve to protect you and provide you with a resilient foundation upon which to face the challenges of life.

Creating a Magical Shield

Part of your task as a Magical Child is to create a physical shield, decorated with the symbols you choose, that will reinforce the energetic shield you will carry on your magical adventure. Make it strong enough so that it retains its shape, yet light enough to carry easily. Make sure you plan well, choosing its shape and then getting all the materials in advance. It can be very satisfying to make a sturdy shield to accompany you on your magical journey. Your shield will eventually provide both physical and energetic protection that you will integrate into your everyday life—a magical tool that you can carry on your magical adventure into the unknown.

Step-by-step instructions for crafting a variety of shields are available in many books and online, including video tutorials. You may also wish to further research the history of shields or designs specific to a culture or clan with whom you feel connected. Think carefully when choosing the shape of your shield. In the context in which it will be used, we recommend that you choose a circular shape. But if a medieval Arthurian knight's shield, a nine-sided shape, or any other design appeals to you, please use it. This will be your own custom-built magical tool, after all! And please note that you're not building a shield that will stop the thrust of a real metal spear. This is rather a shield whose magic will protect against any monster or nasty spell you may meet on your quest.

Shields can be made from a variety of materials. Examples of the base materials include the head of a drum, the lid of a garbage can, or a shaped piece of wood, thick cardboard, or leather. You can then work with paint, dye, markers, feathers, beads, stones, shells, or seeds to adorn it.

While you are building your shield, take time to meditate on the symbols and motifs you will use to decorate it, for this will reflect the energies and qualities you embody on your magical adventure.

Once you have built your shield, you must imbue it with the energy that will bring it alive as your friend and companion on your magical adventure through life. This involves two steps: decorating the shield with symbols of power and dedicating it to your purpose.

Decorating Your Magical Shield

Decorating a power tool is a great creative and magical act. Some people like to do such acts with the support of ceremony. When you are ready to create, try performing a bardic ritual and asking for the help of the Sacred and any suitable beings you feel can support and guide you in the process. You must find your own way in this.

Decorating your shield can take some time. It is important that you discover the most suitable symbols to use on your shield. The design is a sacred mandala; the items that comprise it will remind you of who you are, the qualities you are working with on your magical adventure, and the nature of the magical adventure itself. You can consult your inner Warrior or simply meditate on the subject whenever you feel the time is right. Or you can ask Spirit or your inner Hunter for guidance. Do whatever you need to access this information.

The answer may come all at once, or it may come gradually. It may not even be your destiny to know for sure, and you may simply have to trust that the symbols you choose are the right ones. Or you may get your answers, only to have them change. You can allow this to happen for a while, but, sooner or later, you will have to choose! The process is different for everyone and will mirror part of your unique journey to become a Warrior.

The design you choose may be symmetrical or geometric or something you draw freehand. It may be a medicine wheel, a circle, or a cross dividing a circle, with symbols at the Four Directions and perhaps one at the center. It may be a drawing of a scene depicting an object or a landscape that has particular significance for you. It may include an Awen symbol, a pyramid, a star, your inner Hunter, a power animal, a special species of tree, the planet Earth—in fact, just about anything.

Once you have become clear about the symbols you want to use, you must decide the medium you will use to apply those symbols to the shield. Most people paint their shields, but you can also work with other materials—like sheet metal (brass, copper, nickel, silver, etc), items found in nature, or some form of collage. Paint a layer of varnish or some other transparent protection on top of your design. Research your medium, and be sure that it is waterproof! Many budding Warriors have looked on, dismayed, while the varnish they hoped would protect their creation smudged or completely ruined their valiant efforts.

Dedicating Your Magical Shield

Once you have finished decorating your shield, you must dedicate and activate it. Again, wait until the conditions are perfect for you and the ceremony you wish to perform. Research well, so you know exactly what you want to do and why. Be clear about the being or quality to which you will dedicate your shield. It can be a deity, a quality like freedom, or simply the success of your magical adventure. Be sure to dedicate it at an auspicious time—on your birthday, on a Full Moon, or during an eclipse. Use every opportunity to imbue your magical shield with power.

Be careful choosing the words you use in activating your shield. Make sure they do not have other meanings! Your shield will become a friend, support, protector, reminder, and oasis of awareness for you in the future. It will bring you back to yourself in times of stress, especially when dealing with monsters and nasty things that will try to pull you off balance through fear, emotional extremes, or even overconfidence!

Here is an example of how to dedicate and activate a Warrior's shield. Perform the Bardic Opening Ritual, then give this invocation:

> Dear God, dear Goddess, dear Spirit of these lands, of this place, thank you for being present so strongly this day / evening. I ask for your blessings, your guidance, your protection, and your inspiration in this, my ceremony to dedicate and activate my shield.

Begin your ceremony with these words:

> The purpose of this ceremony is to dedicate and activate
> my new shield. I smudge my new shield so that any old
> energy attached to it falls away and dissolves. Let it be
> renewed and start afresh with its new purpose: to be
> my companion on my new adventure through life, to
> protect, remind, and guide me on my way.
>
> I hold my shield and admire its strength, its beauty,
> and the power it holds. It is a magical tool designed to
> deflect any harmful energy that is directed toward me
> or any that is simply coming my way. It is also a device
> to inform the world of my presence, and the symbols of
> the design represent the energies I am working with on
> my magical adventure. It is my duty to behave in a way
> that harmonizes with the symbols on my shield and to
> develop these qualities to the best of my ability.
>
> I dedicate my shield to the healing and awakening of
> myself and All Beings, for we are All One. May we learn
> to dance in freedom together!
>
> I affirm that my shield is now dedicated!

Once the shield is dedicated, you must activate its power. Begin
with these words, placing the shield on your left or right forearm,
whichever is opposite your dominant hand:

> It is now time to activate my new shield. For the first
> time, in earnest, I imagine myself as a Magical Child
> and Warrior on my magical quest. My shield is part of
> my Warrior self and is now indivisible from me. It is
> both a physical and energetic shield, and adds a whole
> new depth and power to my magical adventure.

The Bardic Book of Becoming

I now embody the qualities and energies of my Warrior's shield. I am fully awake, alert, respectful, and confident. I am a Bard on my magical adventure, and I open myself to develop inside me the behavior of a Spiritual Warrior.

Let my magical shield be activated!

I now imagine myself as a Magical Child and Warrior, my aura complete and whole, and traveling my magical destiny with enthusiasm and confidence.

Repeat the Warrior's affirmation with visualization:

I am awake, my heart is open, and I am a Spiritual Warrior!

I affirm that my shield is now activated!

When you are ready, finish your ceremony by saying:

Now is the time of recall. As the fire dies down, may it be rekindled in my heart.

Complete the ceremony with the Bardic Closing Ritual.

Remember that the physical shield you build is just a manifestation of the energetic protection it provides. This protection is built into your aura and is with you even though your physical shield may be hanging on your wall at home. This energetic shield is an attitude that focuses your mind in a particular way and creates the optimum conditions for success on your magical adventure. It is a shield that will defend you against the enemies or obstacles you will meet on your way. This protection will not simply appear and become effective by itself, however. You must develop it and use it on your journey. Practice is the key!

MAGICAL GATEWAYS

A magical gateway is, literally, a portal that leads into another reality. It sometimes has a physical aspect, but it is usually created by the power of your intent. Creating a magical gateway may seem harmless—a game—but when done properly, it is real—awesomely real. When you enter a magical gateway, you enter the reality intended in its creation. Needless to say, it is very important that you be conscious of what you are doing and why you are doing it! A magical gateway is an expression of your commitment to awaken and embody your own Magical Child. Entering it activates the magical adventure of your life.

When you pass through a magical gateway, a new world greets you. It may seem very similar to the reality you have left, but this new world will be one of magic, commitment, and power. It is a reality that enables you to immerse yourself completely in life, giving you the opportunity to develop yourself to your fullest potential.

Once you have entered this gateway, you must strive to lead a courageous and impeccable life and acquire the skills to perform acts of great power. Imagine that you are entering a world of heroes, heroines, and great deeds and that you are the hero or heroine in your own magical adventure. This gateway will transport you to a reality that can lead you to your truth and your soul.

Always remember that, once you have passed through a magical gateway, you have embarked on your magical adventure!

Entering a Magical Gateway

When you are ready, take a walk in nature. This can be in an area you know or one that is new to you. Walk and enjoy the landscape, keeping a lookout for a place that reminds you of a magical gateway. This may be the space between two vibrant, mature trees, or two rocks, or a tunnel through overhanging trees, or a bridge—whatever fires your imagination. Make sure there is nobody nearby who can disturb you.

Once you have recognized your gateway, approach it with respect. When you are standing in front of it, activate it by imagining it coming alive with light or perhaps a humming sound—whatever seems right and realistic to you. Then, say aloud:

The gateway into my magical adventure is now open!

Pause, and breathe deeply, knowing that you are about to change your life forever. You are leaving the life you have been accustomed to and are about to enter a new world, a world of magic and power where you are the hero or heroine of your own adventure. Say gently:

I now enter my magical adventure!

Step into your new life and acknowledge that you are starting your magical adventure as a Magical Child by saying:

It is done. I am the hero/heroine of my own magical adventure. Blessed be!

When you return from your magical adventure, pass through the gateway backward. Then facing the gateway, visualize the light leaving it. Say:

The gateway is now deactivated!

Visualize the magical gateway dissolving, and then it is gone.

Turn around, and move away from the dissolved gateway. Do not look back. Keep walking and enjoy being the star in your new life as a Magical Child and budding Spiritual Warrior. Also, don't forget to practice using your energetic shield until it becomes second nature and part of your new everyday reality.

Good luck, and may you have great success on your journey! Blessed be!

Part II

THE SPIRIT OF GAIA

Chapter 13

THE FOUR ELEMENTS

In this section of the book, we will explore the four elements. It is appropriate that we do this here, as the elements are an introduction to the wider study of geomancy, the art of communicating with the spirit of Gaia and building meaningful, spiritual relationships with the spirit of the Earth. Druids-in-training are instructed to find an area of land that feels right to them and then to get to know it intimately over time. This location will become their friend and teacher over the years and will reveal hidden sides of itself as the relationship deepens.

One of the first things bards do in their training is to explore the foundations of reality and of physical life on Earth. Thus they study the four elements, the basic building blocks upon which the entire Universe is built.

Druids experience all things as made up of four elements in differing combinations and proportions: Earth, Water, Air, and Fire. Each element corresponds to a Direction, and Spirit is at the center, connecting all together with the spark of life. In the

Northern Hemisphere, Earth corresponds to the North, Water corresponds to the West, Air corresponds to the East, and Fire corresponds to the South. One definition of an element in this context is a fundamental quality that cannot be subdivided. Everything we can name is therefore a combination of these four elements. All things that have solidity, structure, and form contain Earth; all things that flow or have feelings comprise Water; all things that involve sound, thinking, communication, movement, or levity (weightlessness) represent Air; all things that have warmth or energy include Fire.

The four elements are sometimes referred to as "primary matter." When combined, they give rise to our physical Universe in both its visible and invisible aspects. The terms earth, water, air, and fire, when applied to the elements, mean not only physical rocks, pools of water, or flickering flames; they also represent the *potential* of each element. While there is usually one obvious, primary element present in each object or phenomenon, all the others are present in varying proportions.

For example, a burning piece of wood primarily expresses the element of Fire, yet the element of Earth represents its solidity. The element of Air must be added, as fire needs air to burn, and also a little of the element of Water, as there is often residual moisture contained in wood. Moreover, all wood is not created equal. Unseasoned, wet wood *contains* the element of Fire, but unless it has properly dried, the presence of the element of Water may be greater than that of Fire. In this case, the wood may not actually be capable of igniting. The element of Fire is also present in dry, seasoned wood, even if it hasn't actually been set on fire. Until it is ignited, the element of Earth will predominate.

Everything is a mixture of one or more elements, in differing proportions. For instance, herbs and flowers are understood to be manifestations of the Earth element; however, light and leafy herbs, or those with strong scents, are combinations of Earth and Air. Hot spicy plants and cacti are of both Earth and Fire. Aquatic flowers, or flowers growing in marshy conditions, are a mixture of Earth and Water, and roots contain a double dose of Earth. Similarly, candles are physically heavy (Earth element), yet are magical tools of fire (Fire element). By using various colors or scents in their manufacture, the other elements can also be attracted to join in the dance, depending on the ingredients used.

The relationships between the different elements produce very different effects. For instance, each element has a special, mutually beneficial "lover":

- Air combined with Fire creates an inferno.

- Earth provides support, containment, and direction to flowing Water.

Each element also has a "friend" with which it combines harmoniously:

- Air combines with Water to make water vapor and clouds.

- Earth provides foundation and containment on and in which Fire may flourish.

And each element has an "enemy," an equal and opposite, that tends to neutralize it:

- Air is blocked by Earth; Earth is blown away by Air.

- Water extinguishes Fire; Fire evaporates Water.

Combining each element with itself creates extreme conditions:

- Fire joined with Fire produces a firestorm.

- Water joined with Water creates flooding.

- Air joined with Air creates dispersion and extreme ungroundedness.

- Earth combined with Earth produces stolidity and inflexibility.

All of the creations of this world, from trees to cars to mountains, and even the planet itself, are manifestations of the four elements combined in varying proportions. This relationship also applies to human beings. The elemental combination present in individuals determines their energetic makeup, and who and what they are.

A good way to discover your own personal makeup is through the study of the celestial influences present at the time of your birth. These influences can easily be read from an astrological chart. Every planet and house of the zodiac possesses corresponding elemental qualities. By noting which planets are in which house, noting their positional relationships (aspects and transits), and taking into consideration the other celestial influences at your birth, you can discover the strength and proportion of each element in your life. Get your own chart done, and check it out!

Alternatively, you can read about the elements and their correspondences and carefully monitor your reactions to each description. Those with which you feel familiar and most comfortable are usually the elements you embody. Those with which you feel uncomfortable or are untouched by are usually those you lack.

THE HILLS ARE ALIVE . . .

Druids experience everything, from rocks to rainbows, as alive and sentient. This also applies to the elements themselves. In order to understand and learn how to work with these building blocks of the Universe, however, you must build a meaningful relationship with them. The consciousness of each element is called an elemental. These magical beings are ancient and incredibly powerful, yet they are willing to connect and interact with us if we have the right attitude and intent. Consequently, it is important to approach the elements with respect, confidence, and an open heart.

If you make contact with elementals often, they will take notice of you. If they believe you are serious about learning from them, they will start to communicate. Be alert, listen— and respond! Respectful interaction is a sure way to get to know them. Be confident when you interact with them, as they sometimes get agitated when confronted by fear or avoidance. If you feel nervous and are unable to be fully present with them, wait until you are more positive and relaxed.

Do not treat all elementals in the same way, for they are very different types of beings. For instance, consider the issue of play. Air and Fire can be playful and will probably welcome some fun; serious Earth may get grumpy and feel you are being disrespectful if you are flippant; and Water may feel you are entirely missing the point and being totally inappropriate by playing in its delicate and romantic presence. The following chapters will give you summaries of the correspondences and activities that pertain to each element and its elemental.

Observation and personal experience are the best way to learn about the elements at work. Moreover, this is a great way to expand your awareness. Strive to become aware of the way Earth, Water, Air, and Fire dance together and interact every moment of your life to create a unique, ever-changing kaleidoscope of energy—which is you.

A very important principle of awareness is that your outside, so-called objective life is a perfect reflection of your internal reality. In other words, what you observe outside you is actually the outer manifestation of what is happening inside you. It follows, therefore, that, if you wish to know the truth of the moment, you must look inward not outward. Your feelings and bodily sensations are the tools you use to identify and illustrate your invisible, internal reality. So you can become aware of the individual elements of any situation in which you are involved *by becoming conscious of the sensations in and on your own body*. Being aware of and recognizing your sensations is particularly useful in revealing the invisible truth of most situations, especially when you suspect someone is trying to deceive you. This is well illustrated by the expression "trust your gut."

It is easy to do this. Earth tends to generate solid and heavy sensations. Water flows and moves downward to the lowest possible position, channeling feeling and emotions, and is cooling and associated with love and healing. Air encourages levity, lively thoughts, and movement and promotes ungroundedness. Fire heats, tends to move suddenly, initiates, generates enthusiasm and passion, and can be impetuous and unfeeling.

ELEMENTAL RELATIONSHIPS

Druid students work with the elements by building healthy and loving relationships with themselves and with the Universe. Everything a Druid does is motivated by the desire to contact the heart of existence, to explore with love and curiosity, and to increase awareness. When you hold this attitude with the elements, they respond in kind.

Initially, Druids concentrate on each element individually, exploring its qualities both intellectually and experientially, and recording the results in their journals. In this way, they create tables of correspondences that help them observe how the elements manifest in their own personal lives—when they study, when they go for a run, in their relationships, while daydreaming, when they cook. Then they look at how the elements come together in various permutations and combinations relating to specific situations in their lives. The process is not unlike learning a new language. At first it can seem strange and confusing. After enough practice, however, it all comes together and makes sense.

Once students have begun to identify the way in which the elements manifest in their own lives, they perform a series of rituals, formally greeting each elemental in order to initiate conscious, magical relationships with it. In this meeting, they request it to teach them about its qualities and ask if there is anything they can do in return. Relationship is all about love, respect, and energy exchange, after all!

Students then undertake a series of projects that have as their intent the celebration of each element. For instance, for an Earth project, you can honor the element of Earth by finding a physical substance like wood or clay and shaping it into something beautiful. Some examples of this are whittling a piece of wood, molding some clay, erecting a standing stone, or building an altar. For a Water project, you can perform a simple healing ritual, wash your car, install a water feature in your house, or do a water-based meditation.

The first element we will work with here is Earth, as it represents foundation and beginnings. Once we have worked with each element individually, we will gather them all together in ritual and honor their combined dance through both the cosmos and our lives. This we will do in the presence of the Sacred, the presence that permeates everything and breathes life and meaning into matter.

Getting to know and building a loving relationship with the elements is not a very glamorous type of magical work, but it is essential. By its very nature, it is slow and methodical and provides a foundation upon which all other Druidic knowledge is built. In the Ovate and Druid grades, students build a deeper, more dynamic relationship with the four types of elementals. Then matters get decidedly more energetic!

Chapter 14

EARTH

The element of Earth represents the Mother—mater, matter, material—the planet Earth itself. It engenders body and solidity. It provides permanence, stability, and security. Foundation. Reality. Normality. Earth grounds the things you can see and hold, the physical aspects of life, and the process of manifestation. It is your body. It is food. It represents "facts"—those things that can be confirmed by others, by personal experience. Simply put, it is the awesome state of simply being.

In the wheel of the elements, Earth is placed in the North. This is the place of nature, the fruitful Earth, old age, wisdom, and ice and snow. It is also, paradoxically, the midnight sky and the place where the stars twinkle and sing the songs of our spirits in the infinite spaces overhead. Death is also attributed to the North, as winter is the season when vegetation dies, composts, and returns to the Earth. The Sun also seems to die at this time, becoming weak and low in the sky, unable to repel the frost giants that overwhelm the land with ice and snow.

Earth promises purification, grounding, and deep healing. As you walk through the countryside, you experience the healing influences of nature whenever you open your heart to the awesome beauty that surrounds you. You can climb a tree, sunbathe on a large rock, or simply sit down, relax, and daydream. You can meditate, practice gazing and slowing down your thoughts, even go to sleep in a shady, protected place. Simply by enjoying nature, you become healed, purified, and renewed. For a more intense experience of Earth, you can visit and spend time in a cave. There, you are completely surrounded by the Earth.

It is no coincidence that saints and mystics throughout the ages have been drawn to live in caves. For twenty years or so, I used to spend the period from Winter Solstice to just after the New Year in one of the caves I discovered on my travels in the U.K. and abroad. I found it transformational and very healing to replace the frantic holiday mania with the deep peace I found in the solid Earth for a period of two weeks, over the slowest and darkest time of the year. Although I brought candles and a headlamp, I also spent time in the darkness, meditating, fully immersed and at one with the Earth. The grunginess and psychic residue that had accumulated over the entire year dissolved away, and I emerged at the start of the New Year newly born, refreshed, and ready to start a new annual Sun cycle.

Every element offers its own type of healing. Earth is the element that rules the healing of our physical bodies. Types of Earth healing include surgery, massage, chiropractic, herbs, crystals, nutritional therapy in its many forms, acupressure (*shiatsu*), and anything that involves hands-on treatment.

GNOMES

The Earth elementals are called gnomes. They appear in many sizes, from molehills to mountains. Gnomes are the easiest type of elemental to see. You just have to slow down to the speed of the Earth and have a good imagination. Humans can communicate with gnomes more easily than with other elementals because they are the densest—the most like us. They live inside the Earth and don't like exposure or sunlight. They work hard and tend to be quite serious.

Gnomes can be good friends to those who love and work with the Earth. They respect wealth and those who are thrifty and are drawn to those who make the effort to recycle. They appreciate coins, stones, and crystals as gifts. They are also attracted to any work we do to heal the Earth; for example, when we plant trees, garden, pick up litter, or practice geomancy. A friend of mine, a dowser and Earth-healer, was always accompanied by a gnome or two. She could see them perfectly well and gave us blow-by-blow accounts of their often outrageous antics!

Whenever you enter an unhappy, wounded place, request help from the gnomes. Sit quietly for a while and ask them for guidance. It helps if you carry an "Earth healing kit" with you—a special crystal to plant, some dried herbs for smudging, a sacred song or two, ideas for a ceremony, a bag of wildflower seeds, and a musical instrument. Open yourself to guidance and intuit a course of action. Trust yourself and do whatever feels appropriate.

Simply meditating and filling the area with healing energy is usually enough. You may find yourself making a small stone circle when it feels right and then dancing a dance of joy within it!

Allow yourself to be free and creative. Build a cairn, sing a song, play a tune on your flute, say a prayer, make a nature sculpture from items you find nearby, or simply appreciate the beauty of the scenery.

Gnomes help to heal the body and the Earth itself. They can help you break habits that aren't healthy. They will work with you to generate prosperity and abundance. They can assist with any issues concerning work, family, and community.

If you want to make an altar to honor the element of Earth, place it in the northern part of your house or outside to the north of your house. Place a large flat stone somewhere that feels right. If you are inside, use an altar cloth or a combination of brown, green, and black cloths. On the altar, place objects like crystals, rocks, plants, coins, herbs sacred to Earth, moss, a pentagram, horns, or antlers. Cleanse it with smudge and invite the element of Earth and the gnomes to make their home there. Light a candle (with appropriate color and scent) whenever you want to activate your altar for any reason. And keep it clean!

Gratitude is the attitude sacred to Earth. Be thankful for the miraculous gift of life and for the awesome opportunities it presents to you. Celebrate the abundance you experience and spread your good fortune around to enrich everyone you meet!

EARTH CEREMONY

Find a place that strongly embodies the energy of Earth—a quarry, a rocky ravine, a sandpit, or a mountain with lots of exposed rock. It can even be a cave. Visit this place as if on a pilgrimage to the home of the element Earth. Bring an earthy gift like a crystal or a beautiful stone.

When you arrive, find a place that feels right to you. Sit or remain standing and take in the surroundings. Appreciate the beauty of the landscape and allow yourself to be touched by the sheer earthiness that surrounds you. Try to feel the Earth elemental that lives there. In your own words, greet the spirit of the place and the element of Earth. Place your gift in an appropriate spot nearby.

Take some deep breaths and relax. As you breathe in, feel the energy of the Universe entering you, helping you with your ceremony. As you exhale, feel any tensions or uncomfortable feelings drop away into the ground. Feel the energy of Earth supporting you.

Do a simple ceremony to create sacred space, like the one given here:

When you are ready, greet the (imaginary or real) sunrise in the East. Raise your hand and say:

May there be Peace in the East!

Turn to the South, raise your hand, and say:

May there be Peace in the South!

Turn to the West, raise your hand, and say:

May there be Peace in the West!

Turn to the North, raise your hand, and say:

May there be Peace in the North!

Now turn back to face the East and say:

Let there be Peace throughout the whole world!

Pause a few seconds, then say:

> I declare this space sacred and prepared for my
> ceremony!

In your own words, ask the Earth element to be your friend, teacher, and guide into the magic of the elements. Communicate your desire to build a deep relationship with Earth and your intent to use your new powers to help the Earth and all beings. Make sure your words are heartfelt and that you mean what you say. Then close the ceremony by saying:

> Thank you, dear element of Earth, for our new relation-
> ship. Let me manifest healthy and powerful Earth
> energies in my life.

Give another gift to the Earth element—a heart-gift like a poem, a song, a dance, or a prayer. Finally, thank the Four Directions for their support in your ceremony, then say:

> Let my ceremony end in Peace, as in Peace it began.
> Blessed be!

Before speaking or changing the energy of the moment, write down anything you wish to record in your journal. When you are ready, say: "It is done!" Then clap your hands sharply.

EARTH PROJECT

Build an Earth altar. First, choose the location. If not on land you own, it should really be off the beaten track in a place where it won't be seen. Next time you visit this location, search for the perfect place and mark it, possibly with a big stone. Choose a day when the weather is friendly and visit the site with any tools you may need. You can build the altar in one session or in installments.

An altar dedicated to the element of Earth needs to be heavy and solid. Find a large flat stone to act as a table and some smaller stones to lift the table above ground level. This doesn't need to be elaborate. Make it according to your strength and skills. If there are no stones on site, create a mound of dirt, or even find a suitable tree or tree stump. Be creative. And ask the spirit of the place to help you with your project.

Once you have created a physical altar and are pleased with it, you must decorate it. Use whatever you find in the area to demonstrate your love and caring for the Earth. Make patterns with feathers, vines, rocks, shells, bones, flowers, leaves, crystals, moss, pieces of wood—whatever you can find. Spend whatever time you have creating a suitable home for the element, and act impeccably.

When the altar is complete, appreciate your work. Then take out any special personal objects you have brought from home as gifts for the Earth. They can be beautiful stones, crystals, bones, or anything physical and earthy. Finally, place a candle inside a lantern on the altar

When you are ready, light the candle and do a simple ritual to honor the Earth elementals. Invite the gnomes to take up residence in the altar if they wish. Gift them with heartfelt words, a song, music, poetry, a prayer, a dance—whatever makes you feel right. Meditate for a while next to the altar if you wish, radiating peaceful and grounded energies into the structure. Visualize these peaceful, healing energies radiating out from the altar and embracing the entire planet Earth. Do this for as long as it feels comfortable.

Visit the altar whenever you can. Whenever you are there, light a candle and leave gifts like flowers, a song, or a heartfelt prayer. In this way, you will build a powerful and genuine relationship with the element of Earth.

Chapter 15

WATER

Water has many moods. It can be shimmering silver, deep black, turgid brown, crystal clear, cold and gray, and wild foamy green. The diverse realities hidden under its mirror surface challenge us to plunge in and immerse ourselves in the reality of the moment. Will we find deep peace or a tempestuous torrent? Flowing play-fulness or cold gray detachment? Will we be stroked by sensual currents or pummeled by crashing crushing waves?

Until you gather yourself and surrender to the present moment, immersing yourself fully in the currents of life, your destiny will always remain hidden below the surface—an unreachable dream, a life unlived. Only when you let go of what you want or expect life to be will you be presented with the miraculous gift of life in all its glory. At that point, you can know what your destiny truly is and begin to fulfill your purpose here on Earth.

As you explore the waters of life, they reveal themselves to you, from the mightiest oceans to the tiniest capillary in your body. You ride huge ocean swells, body-surf onto exotic sandy beaches, stand under exhilarating waterfalls in green leafy jungles, swim in cold crystal-clear mountain streams, and settle into soft clinging mists above the timberline.

Water has infinite states of being, from icy Arctic oceans to humid sweat lodges. It is soft, healing, and gentle, yet can change to a tree-snapping tsunami in seconds. It is fickle and unpredictable and must never be taken for granted. We humans think we can contain and channel water and that we have everything under control; then a cyclone hits or a dam breaks, and all is swept away

Water is the element generally associated with the West. It is the place where the Sun sets—the time of rest after hard work, the soothing time when we relax and play before going to sleep. It rules those liminal times between true day and true night, between work and sleep, the times when the veils are thin. It is associated with middle to old age, when we settle to enjoy some peace after the struggle to establish our life paths and our long-term relationships, finally owning our own homes, and having weathered the storms of our teenage children.

Water rules the shadowy period between consciousness and sleep when twilight makes the physical world very hard to distinguish. Thus, it is associated with dreams, visions, and illusions, in which everyday reality becomes ephemeral and uncertain.

Whenever you feel lost, confused, despairing, or in emotional pain, take a moment to ground, to center, and to ask Water for guidance. As you do, allow yourself to become aware of your heart. Imagine it is a baby and hold it carefully, lovingly. Rock it gently and tell it that you are looking after it; it is safe now, and you will never allow it to be lost again.

Remember not to look outside yourself for guidance or love. You are the true guide, the loving parent, your own guardian;

you know the way. Allow a sense of peace to come over you and remember that, when your heart is open, you are, in truth, never alone.

The heart and healing are associated with Water. Love is the greatest of the emotions, and many believe that all you need is love. Remember how world-changing those words were in the 1960s? Do you recall the first time you fell in love? How you became ruled by your emotions and started to behave in completely irrational, uncontrolled ways that just weren't a part of the person that you thought you knew?

It is a fact that our physical bodies are comprised of over 60 percent water. The liquid inside us is pushed and pulled by the influences of the Moon, the Sun, and the planets in varying degrees. Women's menstrual cycles are regulated by the Moon and, in many cultures and communities, it is common for all the women to share a common Moon cycle. A poet friend of mine, George Lisi, refers to humans as "water in a skin, ponds that walk the earth." As ponds, we are full, we are empty, we are clean, smelly, murky, and all the rest! It is our destiny as humans to learn to see through the illusion created by our emotional filters to find the eternal, unchanging center that lies within.

Like all other substances on, in, and above the Earth, water is alive and fully sentient. One of its more important properties is that it responds to outside stimuli. Dr. Masaru Emoto and others have researched how water can be programmed to change its internal crystalline structure in resonance with the type of energy in which it is immersed. Thus, it is possible to "heal" polluted water by removing the original polluting source and focusing love on it. This applies to our own bodies as well as the streams and oceans of the world.

Water assumes the shape of the container that surrounds it, whether that is a cup, a lake, a cloud, a human body, or a river. While in this container, it always flows to the lowest possible level. The magical tool associated with Water is the cup or chalice, a symbol that has transformed over time into the Holy Grail, the vessel of divine love, and has come to represent unconditional love, spiritual healing, and the return to wholeness.

One of the major functions of Water in both physical and spiritual applications is its role as a cleanser. We cleanse and purify our bodies, inside and out, with water. We bathe, shower, wash our clothes, and scrub the floors of our homes. Water also cleanses our auras; it can be used in regular psychic hygiene practices. It eliminates any old feelings or psychic residue that may be stuck and need removing. Water is also used in simple house cleansings and, in extreme cases, in exorcisms.

Try this exercise. Soon after you wake up and before you start your day, fill a glass or chalice with water. Contemplate it for a while, knowing it can assume any state you wish, changing itself to align with any type of energy you send to it. Request that the Goddess fill it with blessings and, at the same time, open your heart.

Then say, "All water is sacred" three times and drink the water, following it down, in your imagination, as you swallow it. Feel the Awen fill your entire body. If you like this simple connection with Water and the Sacred, perform it every morning. It is a wonderful way to start the day!

Water has another awesome property that combines both its cleansing action and its capacity for love: forgiveness. Forgiveness allows you to let go of old resentments, loosens stuck emotions and fills the resulting space with love, and gifts you with emotional freedom. Druids work with forgiveness in the Ovate grade as a preparation for shamanic death.

UNDINES

The elementals of Water are called undines. These are flowing, translucent beings that can be imagined as little sparkling movements like the reflection of the Sun or stars on the surface of a lake. They are sentimental and romantic and love those who are in touch with their emotions. Tears, love poetry and songs, scented oils, and perfumes make suitable gifts for these beings.

Ask the undines to help with any matters of love and forgiveness and prayers of well-wishing and healing for yourself or others. They will often manifest in the presence of the person for whom the prayer is made. They are eager to aid anyone interested in healing or cleansing the waters of the world, and they are wonderful allies to have on your journey as a Druid or healer. They also help you work with dreams and visions and in transcending the illusory nature of your human perception. Be warned, however: they are delicate and fragile and will avoid the presence of cruelty and brutality, both overt and covert. If these energies manifest often around you, undines will leave and not return.

When making an altar to honor the element of Water, place it in the western part of your house or outside to the west of your house (or by a pond or brook, in whatever direction). Position a large flat stone where it feels appropriate, then place a glass bowl or chalice on it. Fill the bowl with fresh water from a spring, well, or brook, and float some flowers in it. On the altar, arrange items like shells, flowers, plants, herbs sacred to Water, moss, blue or green or transparent crystals, something that represents a fish or serpent, and appropriate herbal essences.

Smudge the altar and invite the element of Water and the undines to make their home there. Light a candle (with appropriate color and scent) whenever you want to activate your altar. And be sure to keep it clean!

Healing, cleansing, and forgiveness are all actions sacred to Water. Be thankful for the miraculous gift of life and for your health, energy, and well-being. Send your heartfelt prayers outward to share good fortune and health with all beings. Search your heart for anyone toward whom you may feel anger or resentment, and see if you can find any desire inside yourself to heal and forgive. Ask the undines to help if you need some support in doing this.

WATER CEREMONY

Find a location that strongly embodies the energy of Water—a brook, a lake, a beach, a waterfall, a river, or an ocean. When you feel ready, visit this place as if on a pilgrimage to the home of the element of Water. Bring a gift like a crystal, a beautiful green or blue stone, or some fresh spring water that you have blessed.

When you arrive, find a spot that feels right to you, sit or remain standing, and face the water. Appreciate the beauty and vitality of the landscape, and allow yourself to be touched by the powerful Water energies that abide in this place. Try to feel the Water elemental that lives there and gauge its mood. In your own words, greet the spirit of the place and the element of Water. Place your gift in or close to the body of water.

Dip your ring finger—your Sun finger—into the water and bless yourself by touching your brow and heart. Take some deep breaths and relax. As you breathe in, feel the energy of the Universe enter you, helping you with your ceremony. As you exhale, feel any tensions or uncomfortable feelings drop away into the ground. Feel the energy of Earth supporting you.

When you are ready, greet the (imaginary or real) sunrise in the East. Raise your hand and say:

May there be Peace in the East!

Turn to the South, raise your hand, and say:

May there be Peace in the South!

Turn to the West, raise your hand, and say:

May there be Peace in the West!

Turn to the North, raise your hand, and say:

May there be Peace in the North!

Now turn to face the Water and say:

Let there be Peace throughout the whole world!

Pause a few seconds, then say:

I declare this space sacred and prepared for my
    ceremony!

In your own words, request that the Water element be your friend, teacher, and guide into the magic of the elements. Communicate your desire to build a deep relationship with Water, and share your intent to use your new powers to help the planet Earth and all beings. Make sure your words are heartfelt and that you mean them. Then say:

Thank you, dear element of Water, for our new relationship. Let me manifest healthy and powerful Water
energies in my life.

Give another gift to the Water element—a heart-gift like a poem,
a song, a dance, or a prayer. Finally, thank the four Directions for
their support in your ceremony. Then say:

Let my ceremony end in Peace, as in Peace it began.
Blessed be!

Before speaking or changing the energy of the moment, write
down anything you wish to record in your journal. When you are
ready, say: "It is done!" Then clap your hands sharply.

WATER PROJECT

Fill your bathtub with hot water, scent it with your favorite essential oils or bath salts, and light a candle. Turn the lights off and
lower yourself into the water. Feel the water touch your skin and
flow up your body. Feel the ripples in the water as it responds to
your breathing. Close your eyes and sink lower until just your
nose is above the surface. Relax as fully as you can and be still.
Then listen for your heartbeat. Ask the Mother to let you feel her
love, and open yourself to receive it. Imagine that you are in the
Mother's womb—feel the dark, peaceful, watery nourishment of
her cauldron, where life begins.

Let your thoughts wander toward those for whom you hold
negative feelings. This may be one or both parents, a sibling or
relative, or anyone you feel has hurt you in any way. See if you
can remain in your loving, warm, and relaxed space, and try to
see these fellow beings as essentially human, with all the strengths

and weaknesses we as a species embody. Understand that they, like all of us, are struggling to love and be loved and are trying to deal with the vicissitudes of life as best they can.

The fact that these individuals were able to do whatever they did to you makes you realize that they are lost and unhappy. See if you can forgive them for their speech and actions and wish them healing and love. Only do this if you truly feel it. But realize that, as long as you hold resentment against them, a part of you will remain stuck until you are finally ready to let it go. If it is difficult to forgive and forget, do it anyway as an expression of love for yourself. Let go of useless hurt and resentment, for they create prisons from which it is difficult to escape. Feel empowered to give yourself the awesome gift of freedom!

If you cannot forgive at this time, make a strong commitment that you will prepare yourself to forgive and let go of your hurt at the right time.

When you are ready, hum a lullaby into the water. Hear your voice resonate through the water, and imagine it is the Great Mother herself singing her love to you. Keep singing and breathing for as long as you feel comfortable and safe, until you are surrounded and permeated by a sense of her love.

Blessed be!

Chapter 16

AIR

Of all the essential ingredients for life, air—breath—is the most immediate and vital. Without oxygen, our lives would be snuffed out like candles in the wind in a fleeting few minutes. With this in mind, take a deep breath into your lungs, and then exhale. Take a moment to ponder the mystery of this ocean of air in which we are immersed and consider how delicate and precious it is. Humans and animals breathe in the air and exhale carbon dioxide. Our cousins, the plants, take in the carbon dioxide and use it to trap the energy of the Sun. When we eat them, we extract this energy. Plants then give off oxygen, and so the cycle of life continues, giving and receiving so that we all can live symbiotically, in harmony with one another.

The element of Air is associated with the East. This is where the Sun rises, so this thinnest and most ethereal of the elements is associated with initiation and new beginnings. It is associated with springtime and the wonder and curiosity of childhood.

Think of the joy you feel as the sky lightens in the East and the coldness and loneliness of the night are soon to end. Think of the sense of imminence you feel as you see the clouds take on the glorious colors of the beginning of a new day. The shadows flee the swords of light and your heart fills with the promise of the new day. We feel the same sense of potential, of awe at the beauty of a life beginning, when we hear the cry of a newborn babe or when the winds of spring blow the scents of the thaw and the bursting blossoms our way.

The element of Air is associated with the sense of smell. While there are scents we associate with each of the elements, the scents of spring flowers come to mind when we think of Air. Air also rules the act of smudging—cleansing or purifying with the smoldering scent of sage, lavender, lemongrass, cedar, and pine. Incense is one of the important magical tools of the East and of Air.

Think for a moment about how scent can affect your mood, your state of mind. How does the memory of cinnamon make you feel? Perhaps you remember the apple pies your mother used to make, so it makes you feel loved and nurtured. And roses. Do they conjure up late summer evenings? Past and present romances? Does lavender take you back to your grandmother's house and give you a sense of age and cleanliness? Frankincense and myrrh—churches and sacred spaces?

The element of Air is also associated with music, for sound is transmitted through vibrating airwaves. Music has profoundly changed the consciousness of humans throughout the ages and is an expression of our inner souls. Air carries the songs of the wind rustling in the trees, of the songbirds, of flutes and whistles, and of our own voices raised in song.

The Bardic Book of Becoming

To soak up the power of Air, get out of bed early enough to greet the dawn. Make yourself comfortable and *really* listen to the birds as they sing their joy at the coming light of a new day. In fact, take part if you wish. Call back to the birds. Perhaps offer them some seed. Really feel the joy of interacting with these creatures of Air at the time when their energy is at its highest.

Angels are especially associated with Air, although there are angels specifically associated with each of the elements. The Archangel who is considered the Guardian of Air is Raphael, whose name means "Healer of God." He is robed in gold, yellow, and blue and carries a caduceus, a wand entwined by two serpents that is used as a symbol of healing. He rules science, knowledge, compassion, and healing. Another being who carries a caduceus, of course, is Mercury, messenger of the gods. Mercury is a Guardian of Air who rules intellect, verbal expression, science, synthesis, and research. He has wings at his ankles.

Air rules the mind and mental activity. It rules clarity and clear thought; any meditation or discipline that purifies the mind is Air's friend. Ideas and intuitions that come "out of the blue" are its children. Synthesizing different ideas and concepts and making good decisions are signs of healthy Air. Communication in all its aspects is also ruled by Air, from body language, to speech and writing, to teaching and poetry, to conflict resolution. Anything to do with lightness or levity, or with making music, is ruled by Air.

SYLPHS

The elementals associated with Air are called sylphs, and they can often be seen as movement out of the corner of your eye. They are very playful and make themselves known in many ways—by gently stroking naked skin in the summer or by rustling dried leaves in the fall. Sometimes they are called fairies, and many children can see them. I sometimes see them as little flashes of light and feel them as a subtle magical presence. When I feel them nearby, I often play my flute for them, and it makes me very happy to sense their delight. They enjoy dancing in ways that make the invisible visible—for instance, making the leaves swirl in the fall or creating miniature tornados that pick up dust in the summer and powdery snow in the winter.

Breathing exercises are invaluable for developing the ability to use Air energy and power in your magical work. If you want to meet the sylphs, find a hilltop or place outside in nature where the wind loves to spin and whirl, sweeping clean the landscape of dust and leaves and tousling your hair. Simply enjoy their vitality and beauty. Then, if you feel inspired, offer them a gift like playing your flute, or singing a song, or reciting a poem, or dancing a dance, or wafting a scent. Have fun and play with them!

To honor the element of Air and the sylphs, make an altar to the east of your house, either inside or out. Drape it and decorate it in blues, yellows, and white. Place appropriate objects onto it— feathers, blue or yellow wispy flowers, "helicopter seeds" from trees, butterfly wings, flutes, pale blue stones, incense, and herbs sacred to Air. Invite the sylphs to make the altar their home. Activate the candles and/or incense whenever you read, write, or study—or simply when you are inspired to do so.

AIR CEREMONY

Find a place that strongly suggests the energy of Air. This can be a high, exposed location like the top of a hill or mesa or a mountain above the timberline. It can even be in the boughs of a tall tree. Once you have found a suitable place to meet and honor Air, make your preparations. You will need a journal, a gift (a beautiful feather or a prayer or poem written on some something biodegradable like a dry leaf), and yourself. At a time of your choosing, possibly when there is a breeze or even a brisk wind, visit this place in the spirit of pilgrimage, knowing you are in the process of fulfilling a sacred task.

When you arrive, take in the surroundings. Appreciate the beauty of the landscape and allow yourself to be touched by the vitality of the element of Air in its place of power. Feel the Air elemental that lives there, and greet it.

Take some deep breaths and relax. As you breathe in, feel the energy of the Universe enter you, helping you with your cere-mony. As you exhale, feel any stress or tensions drop away into the ground. Feel the energy of the Earth supporting you.

When you are ready, greet the (imaginary or real) sunrise in the East. Raise your hand and say:

May there be Peace in the East!

Turn to the South, raise your hand, and say:

May there be Peace in the South!

Turn to the West, raise your hand, and say:

May there be Peace in the West!

Turn to the North, raise your hand, and say:

May there be Peace in the North!

Now turn to face the Direction that feels best to you and say:

Let there be Peace throughout the whole world!

Pause a few seconds, then say:

I declare this space sacred and prepared for my
ceremony!

In your own words, request the element of Air to be your friend, teacher, and guide into the magic of the elements. Communicate your desire to build a deep relationship with Air and your intent to use your new powers to help the planet Earth and all beings.

Make sure your words are heartfelt and that you mean what you say. Throw your gift up into the air, and watch as the breeze accepts it and carries it away. Then say:

Thank you, dear element of Air, for our new relationship. Let me manifest healthy and powerful Air
energies in my life.

Now open your heart and go deep inside. Access the part of you that wants to come fully alive, that yearns to transform you into the human you truly want to become—a whole being of empowerment and authenticity. Contemplate the vision of your future self, and get clear about it. Ask inspiration and creation to come to you, so that you may put into words your dream of becoming.

When you are ready, speak your truth. Share with Air your feelings about your life, about the gifts you have received and any wounds you have suffered. Then state aloud your vision of the future. State your purpose in life and what you are willing to do and to sacrifice in order that your dreams may come to pass. Speak with feeling and passion, for this is your chance to vibrate the web of life with the power of your words and clearly communicate what is gestating within your heart.

Your words are your instrument of creation, so find the courage and clarity to use them in the way Spirit has intended. Try to speak succinctly and to the point. Don't ramble, as this invites unconsciousness and dissipates power very quickly. When you are finished, pause a while to make sure there is nothing more to express, then say:

I have spoken!

Pause for a few moments more, and feel what you have done, what you have set in motion. Finally, thank the four Directions for their support in your ceremony. Then say:

Let my ceremony end in Peace, as in Peace it began.
Blessed be!

Before speaking again, or changing the energy of the moment, write down anything you wish to record in your journal. When you are ready, say: "It is done!" Then clap your hands sharply.

AIR PROJECT

Collect feathers and several types of colorful, light material that can be moved easily by the breeze. Stay alert when you walk in nature, or even in town, for there are feathers everywhere. When you feel you have collected enough—perhaps three dozen or so—search for a tree that stands out from its brothers and sisters as something special, one that wants to play. It is probably best to choose a deciduous tree, as it is easier to attach dangly things to its branches. This tree may be standing close to a special feature in the landscape like a spring, a well, a large rock, a waterfall, or a pool. Or it may be standing alone in an exposed place.

When you find the right tree, spend time with it, enjoying its uniqueness and companionship. Ask it respectfully if you can work with it in the spirit of play and in honor of the Sacred. Explain that you wish to create, with it, a living altar to celebrate the element of Air. If you feel right about your request, or even receive a sign like a bird appearing or singing, or feel a touch from the wind, then you know you have permission. If you have any negative feelings, thank the tree and move on until you find one that wants to play.

At home, prepare the offerings you will hang from the tree's branches. You can also do this outside close to your chosen tree if the air is still. You will need your collection of feathers and light dangly things, strong twine or string, a tube of superglue, and scissors or a knife. Cut the string into lengths of about eighteen inches and tie one end of each piece to the shaft of each feather or dangly thing. If you want to, you can place a drop of super-glue onto the string to make sure the objects don't fly away in the wind. When you are done, store the items safely until you need them.

Choose a dry day when a breeze is blowing. Greet the tree, then tie the feathers and offerings to its branches so that they can hang and move without getting tangled in other small branches or leaves. If there are any small obstructions in the way, ask the tree if you can remove them. If the answer is yes, cut them with a sharp knife or pruning saw. Place the feathers and other bits equally around the tree so that it feels balanced

When you have completed dressing the tree, stand back and admire how Air dances and plays with the tree and the offerings hanging from it. Notice how your actions have created beauty and have made the invisible breeze visible. How do you feel when you look at your creation?

If you wish, sing a song or chant, and speak to the Air elemental. In your own words, share your feelings, your hopes, and your desires. Express gratitude for the life you have been given, and give thanks to nature for its beauty and power. Be sure to speak clearly, concisely, and powerfully. Return whenever you feel the time is right, greeting the tree and the element of Air. Be sure to bring a gift like a poem, a song, a prayer, a dance, or some incense.

Chapter 17

FIRE

The element of Fire is the most active, self-motivated, high spir-ited, and animated of all the elements. The Fire element is our basic life force, the sentient power of our energy bodies, and the background energy that drives the Universe. People and situa-tions blessed by Fire bring joy, color, energy, and sass to life. Fire is active, dynamic, passionate, humorous, courageous, enthusias-tic, transformative, inspirational, and positive. It fuels creativity, spontaneity, and self-empowerment and engenders the fires of freedom and authenticity.

The Sun is our primary source of Fire as we spiral through space and time on our home world, spaceship Earth. It is our star, bestowing its cosmic gift of life upon us throughout eternity. Its thermonuclear core produces unimaginable amounts of Fire energy that radiate outward into the cold reaches of space. We experience it shining like a diamond above our heads, giving us the light and heat necessary to prosper on our paradise planet. Without it, life as we know it would be impossible.

The miracle of photosynthesis enables all plants and trees to convert the Sun's Fire energy into growth, producing food for all animals, including us. Everything under the Sun is interconnected in an intimate symbiotic relationship with all other things; the health of the whole ecosystem called Earth is totally dependent on it. From the Sun to the tiniest micro-organism, all things are sentient and occupy different levels of consciousness. We keep ourselves at an optimum level of energy by building a healthy and harmonious relationship with the Sun, and with the element of Fire.

Fire is associated with the South, where the Sun is at its most powerful. From the northern hemisphere, it is in this direction that the tropics, jungles, and deserts of the planet lie. South is where the Sun shines at its zenith at midday. Fire is also associated with summer, when the Sun is at its hottest. In the summer, we witness the grains and fruits ripening, providing us with the food needed to live and grow. Summer, and thus Fire, is associated with young adulthood, that time of life when we generate and expend huge amounts of energy establishing our careers, building our homes, and generating enough sexual energy to find suitable partners with whom we will create children. Passion is hot!

Movement is one of the qualities of Fire. The faster the movement, the greater the heat—and vice versa. This is why dancing is one of the most effective ways to raise energy and change levels of consciousness. It keeps us grounded while our energy levels increase safely. Dance is a wonderful, natural way to experience ecstasy, dissolve blockages, and express our inner creativity. Dance also pulls people together into the same rhythm, creating a harmonious interaction of body and soul. Moving together as one in sacred space creates a strong and healthy community.

Magical techniques associated with Fire are candle magic, the burning of sacred substances like herbs and particular types of wood, ceremonies requiring fire like sweat lodges, and all techniques involving the energy body—*poi* (fire juggling), fire dancing, and walking on live coals. Fire heals by getting things moving. It initiates new impulses and new directions. It helps us break through inertia, apathy, stagnation, depression, intellectualization, shyness, and the paralysis of fear.

Agnihotra is a ceremony that honors Agni, god of Fire, by offering him gifts. These gifts may be physical in nature—specially harvested and prepared wood, grains, or fine foods, for example—or they can be gifts of the heart, like prayers, songs, a specially composed poem, or a dance. An interesting and beneficial by-product of performing Agnihotra is its power to reduce pollution in the atmosphere and in the surrounding landscape.

Fire corresponds with the will, the force within us that we focus and develop in order to manifest our hearts' desires. It dissolves and overcomes blockages and obstacles in our path; it inspires us and helps us motivate others to undertake common goals. Despite their so-called "negative" associations, anger, frustration, and trauma can be extremely effective catalysts that activate our wills. With this Fire energy available to us, and if we are able to rise to the occasion, miracles are possible. It is said that the best circumstances for healing and transformation are acts of survival.

The magical tool associated with Fire is the wand, which helps to project the energy of magicians outward in order to manifest their intentions. Dedicated, determined effort with a wand can develop the will to an extraordinary degree, but it requires strong motivation and a lot of practice. Once you have successfully completed wand training, the magical art of manifestation becomes second nature to you.

Magicians and energy workers have always used Fire and light for protection. There are many techniques to create effective magical protection around a space or a person. These are grounded in the principle that protection works best when we are alert and aware. They often include setting up an "alarm system" to signal whenever a boundary has been transgressed, sometimes even setting off fiery "electric fence" warnings to the entity that is attempting to trespass or invade. These techniques often succeed because of what I call "the umbrella factor"—if you carry an umbrella, it rarely rains!

The shadow side of Fire is terrifying. Fire has an all-consuming hunger that is insatiable while there is still fuel to burn. Warriors, who are trained to work specifically with the element of Fire, therefore require considerable solidity, sobriety, and control; otherwise Fire can swiftly spiral out of control, consuming everything in its path. When working with Fire, you must be fully grounded and must carry water, both physical and energetic, at all times—and be ready to apply it if it becomes necessary. There was a period in my life when I often lost control of my Fire energy, with alarming results. I found it very helpful to carry a small bottle of water around with me in my shoulder bag. Its mere presence brought balance to my life and helped to cool down my Fire energies.

SALAMANDERS

The Fire elementals are called salamanders. They are brilliant creatures of pure energy that can be seen dancing in flames.

They love people who possess and express Warrior energy and will support them on their paths, helping them face their fears, move through obstacles, and find their wholeness. They will help anyone demonstrating courage, authenticity, and honesty and will always support leaders who live their lives as examples to others. They offer us magical protection and willingly share their energy with energy workers like shamans and Druids. But woe betide anyone attempting to interact with them if they are nervous, timid, disrespectful, or disempowered! If you display fear, are disrespectful, or lack confidence in the presence of a salamander, it will bite!

Salamanders enjoy dancing in the flames of a fire—the larger, the better—and appreciate the gift of acts of courage most. To communicate with them, *make lots of fires* and invite them out to play! Research the types of wood that burn hottest and brightest and ones that have magical or healing properties. Use them skillfully and consciously.

To make and dedicate an altar to the beings of Fire, make it in the southern part of your house. Decorate it in reds, yellows, and oranges. Burn candles; find and display snakeskins and sand; collect red, yellow, and white stones and anything with fiery colors.

Invite the Fire element and the salamanders to make their new home in the altar. Whenever you want to communicate with them, light one or more candles on the altar and interact with your fiery guests with your own inner Fire, will, and imagination. Learn some Fire songs and chants, and dance with the flames. The best type of outside altar is, naturally, a fire pit. Treat it impeccably, with respect, and keep it clean. And dance well!

FIRE CEREMONY

Find a place where you can safely make a fire. This can be in your back yard, in a friendly fire pit, at a camping ground, in a quarry or a sandpit, or on a mountain with lots of exposed rock. It can even be in a cave. There are even some areas of beach where visitors are allowed to make fires. Just be sure you work in an open area where there are no flammable structures and no undergrowth or vegetation nearby. If you make your fire somewhere that is not your own property, either get permission from the landowner or choose a location where you will not be seen.

Don't rush the ceremony; prepare well. Choose your wood consciously, in varied thicknesses between matchstick size and the thickness of your finger. How long do you want your fire to burn? Prepare and carry the appropriate amount of firewood. Be clear about the type of wood you want to burn, for each tree has a unique personality and quality. The wood must be seasoned and dry. If there are any birch trees nearby, collect some birch bark (without killing the tree). Birch bark makes an efficient, sweet-smelling, and spectacular way to start your fire.

When you have made your preparations, choose a dry day. As you approach the place where you will connect with Fire, cultivate an attitude of pilgrimage. Your journey is a sacred one, and you must act accordingly. Bring an appropriate gift or gifts—a flower, some special incense, an organic item of food or grain, a poem or prayer written on special paper, or something beautiful and burnable.

When you arrive, greet the spirit of the place and share the intent of your visit with it. Sit down or remain standing, and take in the surroundings. Quiet your thoughts, open your heart, and appreciate the beauty of the landscape. Feel grateful to be alive and to be touched by magic and the spirit of healing.

When you are ready to start your ceremony, take some deep breaths and relax. As you breathe in, feel the energy of the Universe enter you, helping you with your intention. As you exhale, feel any tensions or uncomfortable feelings drop away into the ground. Feel the energy of Earth supporting you. Stand up and greet the (imaginary or real) sunrise in the East. Raise your hand and say:

May there be Peace in the East!

Turn to the South, raise your hand, and say:

May there be Peace in the South!

Turn to the West, raise your hand, and say:

May there be Peace in the West!

Turn to the North, raise your hand, and say:

May there be Peace in the North!

Now turn back to face the East and say:

Let there be Peace throughout the whole world!

Pause a few seconds, then say:

I declare this space sacred and prepared for my
ceremony!

Sit down, facing the Direction that feels best. In your own words, aloud, ask the Fire element to be your friend, teacher, and guide. Communicate your desire to build a deeper, more magical relationship with Fire and your intent to use your new powers to help and further sacred Fire on Earth. Make sure your words are heartfelt and that you mean what you say.

Start with building a fire pit. Find some suitable-sized stones—perhaps fist-sized—and place them in a circle. This creates an earthy space with strong boundaries within which your fire will burn. Once you are satisfied with your efforts, build the fire. You are building a suitable home for a Fire elemental, so create a space where it will be happy and burn well.

Start with the birch bark, and lay the thinnest kindling on top of it. Then gradually place thicker pieces of wood around the kindling in a teepee shape. Be careful to leave a small gap in the structure of kindling so that you can easily light the fire. Make sure the gap faces the direction from which the breeze is coming so that the Air spirits can help with ignition.

When you are satisfied with your efforts, light the fire by igniting the birch bark. Watch with wonder and curiosity as your fire ignites and grows, as if it were alive. If it needs any encouragement, blow on it or add some small pieces of wood to help it grow happily and healthily.

When the fire is burning happily, give your physical gift to the Fire elemental who is now occupying the Fire temple you have just made. Watch how Fire accepts your offering, consuming its magic like soul food. When you are ready, and the fire is burning well, say:

> Thank you, dear element of Fire, for our new relationship. Let me manifest healthy and powerful Fire energies in my life.

After a short period of contemplation, offer your heart-gift to the Fire—a poem, a song, a dance, or a prayer. Then sit in vigil with

The Bardic Book of Becoming

the Fire element, companionably, simply gazing into the flames in a curious and friendly fashion, until most of the wood has been consumed and the flames start to die down.

Thank the Four Directions for their support in your ceremony, then say:

Let my ceremony end in Peace, as in Peace it began.
Blessed be!

Before speaking, or changing the energy of the moment, write down anything you wish to record in your journal. When you are ready, say: "It is done!" Then clap your hands sharply.

Make sure that your fire is completely extinguished before leaving the site.

FIRE PROJECT

To send energy to someone (it could be you) over a period of a month, light a candle every day with a prayer. Your target should be the same throughout the month, because the intent of this ceremony is to experience the power of Fire and prayer growing through repetition.

Buy some tea lights—forty should do. Get a small glass, just big enough for a single tea light. Then make a small altar somewhere in your house, in a place where it won't be disturbed by a child or curious pet—perhaps on a windowsill in the kitchen or bedroom.

Contemplate where you wish to send Fire energy. Remember, this may be yourself. Perhaps you are ill and need some extra energy. Perhaps you need some support to start or complete a project. Perhaps you want to experience the discipline and energy of working with Fire for a month. Or it may be that a friend or relative is ill, or someone you know needs energy at this time. Perhaps a friend is about to give birth or about to go into the hospital for an operation.

Or you may want to direct your prayers to nature, to a place where there is uncontrolled felling of trees or a huge forest fire, or damage done by fracking, or a climate gone crazy. Maybe there has been an earthquake somewhere. You get the idea.

Start, if possible, on the New Moon. And try to perform your ceremony at the same time every day. On the day you have decided to start, be very clear where you want to send the energy. Stand close to the altar and visualize your "target." Say a few words to describe the intent of your ceremony. Then light the candle, knowing you are calling the energy of Fire. Say a few words to welcome Fire into your space. Wait a while, imagining the energy building. When it feels right, say something like: "It is done!" or "Make it so!" or "Blessed be!" Then imagine your prayer winging its way to the target, powered by the element of Fire.

Thank Fire and Spirit for bringing magic into your life and for healing and supporting the target of your prayers. Let the candle burn down, making sure it is safe, and let it remind you of your healing project. Then place a new tea light in the glass and repeat the ceremony each day until the next New Moon.

When the month's ceremony is complete, give thanks for this opportunity to make good magic and bless your target, whoever or whatever it may be. Thank Fire for its help and support.

This can be a one-time ceremony, or it can become a regular event in your life.

The Bardic Book of Becoming

Chapter 18

SPIRIT DANCER

According to the principles of geomancy, the place where we are always represents the center of the Universe. Here, the four elements can be visualized as surrounding us on a horizontal plane, with Earth in the North, Water in the West, Air in the East, and Fire in the South. This may be different depending on the culture or tradition you follow and depending on the hemisphere you are in. Spirit is understood to be at home Above, and health manifests when there is unhindered movement between Above and Below. In practice, Spirit is already fully merged with Earth and interacts healthily with her—if left alone. The strange and unhealthy relationship humans have with their own spirits and with the Earth has thrown everything into disarray, however, and people with awareness are constantly attempting to balance this disharmonious state of affairs.

Spirit is the element of connection, healing, unity, love, fulfillment, empowerment, at-Onement, pure being, the Sacred, and presence. The word "spirit" is interchangeable with the word "power" in this context. Earth is fundamental and solid; the presence of Spirit brings Earth, or matter, to life. When Spirit flows to Earth, the Sacred is born. Harmony, joy, and delight then fill all beings.

Spirit has always been seen as Fire, on a higher frequency or vibration than physical fire. Spirit Fire powers our energy bodies, our auras. Our chakras do much the same job for our auras that our physical organs do for our corporeal bodies. The ancient Egyptians "saw" the Sun as occupying the same space as the crown chakra. They envisioned rays of light and energy descending from the crown, radiating down through the aura, bestowing life and connecting us to the infinite energy and consciousness of the Sun.

Eastern yogis experience *kundalini*, the goddess of life force and sexual power, as a sacred serpent that lies curled at the base of the spine. When this serpent is quiescent, it sleeps, and we operate at "normal" power. Whenever it awakens, however, this serpent rises up the spine, activating each chakra it reaches. At these times, we experience intense surges of energy as each chakra expands and radiates power. When this happens, our entire aura grows and glows with increased awareness and sexuality, and we are swept into ecstasy.

Druids experience an energy similar to kundalini. Instead of a serpent, however, they experience a dragon that activates the chakras as it ascends through the various energy levels toward the crown. This dragon's name is Draco, Ddraig, or Dracolini. This is one of the reasons why dragons often appear in Druid life and training. Dragons are ancient magical beings that look like serpents with wings, after all!

This type of energy activation is both desired and feared by yogis. When your inner energetic channels have been prepared by meditation and regular spiritual practice, kundalini connects you with the godhead. This is experienced as ecstasy, enlightenment, and ultimate empowerment. If kundalini rises before you are ready, before the channels are open and prepared, however, it can be compared to a huge surge of electricity trying to flow along a small and inadequate copper wire. This once happened to me. It was terrifying and damaging, and it burnt out my energetic circuits for a long time afterward. Aware of its potential destructive power, Druids learn how to activate this natural force in gentle, balanced ways. In this way, they increase their Fire energy, which in turn provides the power to heal, transform, and grow.

Without Spirit, the four elements are lifeless—meaningless and empty—representing only the physical world, one half of the duality that is the nature of life on Earth. At present, the majority of humans are unconscious of the need for balance between Earth and Spirit. Until human awareness reaches critical mass, there will always be a preponderance of darkness in the world. To create wholeness and harmony on Earth, we have to invite Spirit to enter our lives and merge with our physical world.

In your exploration of the elements, the final stage must be the act of uniting the polarities of Spirit and Earth inside yourself, thus eradicating duality and creating the conditions that will breathe vitality and purpose into your life. To become a fully conscious being, to fully manifest the Sacred, you must express your authenticity, your unique individual soul, on Earth. This happens through dance.

Dance is a magical act that brings life, movement, and creativity to the world, uniting all beings and all existences. One of the greatest achievements for Druids is the ability to act spontaneously, thus becoming pure, open channels for human creativity. Bards combine Spirit and dance to express and celebrate the parts of the Great Spirit their souls embody, thus manifesting their unique beingness, and the Sacred here on Earth.

PREPARING FOR SPIRIT

For this ceremony, you will need your journal and a pen. Bring a candle in a lantern and matches or a lighter. Choose a place that feels particularly sacred to you. This can be indoors at home or outside in your backyard. The most energetic place will probably be an area of land that you are getting to know in your geomancy practice. It is a wonderful thing to share your sacred journey with the spirit of the land.

If you feel confident enough, do this ceremony on a moonless night, when the stars are shining brightly through the void. Make sure to bring a flashlight so you can see where you are going. Or you can perform the ceremony during the day and imagine it is a starry, starry night as you meditate.

At your chosen place, clear a small area about ten feet in diameter. Light your candle and place the lantern to the side of the area. Enter your circle and face whatever Direction feels best. Then stand still a while, relaxing and tuning in to the land. Appreciate the peace and beauty that surrounds you. How do you feel?

When you are ready, take some deep yet gentle breaths, and relax. As you breathe in, feel the energy of the Universe enter you, helping you with your ceremony. As you exhale, feel any tensions or stress dropping away from you into the ground. Feel the energy of Earth supporting you.

Greet the (imaginary or real) sunrise in the East. Raise your hand and say:

May there be Peace in the East!

Turn to the South, raise your hand, and say:

May there be Peace in the South!

Turn to the West, raise your hand, and say:

May there be Peace in the West!

Turn to the North, raise your hand, and say:

May there be Peace in the North!

Now turn back to face the East and say:

Let there be Peace throughout the whole world!

Pause a few seconds, then say:

I declare this space sacred and prepared for my
ceremony!

Sit down, facing the Direction that feels best to you. In your own words, aloud, ask your inner Spirit Dancer to be your friend, teacher, and guide. Communicate your desire to build a deeper, more magical relationship with Spirit and your intent to learn how to dance with the elements to celebrate and manifest the Sacred on Earth. Make sure your words are heartfelt and that you mean what you say. Then say:

Dear God, dear Goddess, dear Spirit, dear Sacred Dancer,
please enter this space and share your blessings.

Contemplate the candle. The flame represents Spirit; its flickering represents the dance. Appreciate the warmth and light it radiates into your space. Gaze at the candle for about half a minute. *Really* see it as Spirit Dancer, as it expresses, through Fire and movement, the reality of the moment.

In whatever way feels right to you, journey to your sacred grove. Visualize yourself sitting at the center of your special, sacred place. Greet the beings that live there, and share your love and gratitude for their supportive and magical presence. Feel the strength, protection, and vitality that surround you. Feel the Earth below you. Feel the infinite spaces above you. Notice the health and aliveness of your grove.

Now look about you and locate some sort of Spirit feature in your grove. This may be a guide, a fabulous animal, a light, a feeling, a sense, a crystal channeling Spirit, an angel, a rainbow, a special flower—whatever your imagination produces for you. If you cannot find any object or being that symbolizes Spirit to you, create one.

Enjoy the presence of Spirit for a while. Then imagine above you the realms of Spirit, and sense below you the center of the Earth. Witness yourself sitting on the surface of the Earth, connecting the two. Pause for a few seconds, then say:

> I now affirm my true nature. I am a bridge connecting
> Spirit and Earth. From this moment on, all I see and
> touch I make Sacred.

CONNECTING WITH SPIRIT

If the Earth has physical mass, weight, and distance that can be measured, then Spirit is infinity. Connecting with the vast, immeasurable spaces in the Universe brings you into alignment with Spirit. Here is an exercise that can help you experience the contrast between everyday consciousness and the presence of Spirit.

Imagine you are standing on the Earth's surface on a sunny day. You are surrounded by recognizable landscapes filled with trees, houses, mountains, plains, and roads. Everything you see has length, width, and height; everything is familiar and known, enclosed by the blue sky that envelops our wonderful planet. It is all so normal—something you can easily handle. This is your familiar, finite, everyday consciousness.

After a brief pause, imagine that the Sun is setting, plunging the world into darkness; the stars become visible. The deep blue enveloping sky dissolves; a vast space opens up above you and you realize you can touch infinity. You become aware that the visible stars above your head are scattered through space in three dimensions, occupying spaces unimaginably distant. You are still standing on Earth, however, and you feel comforting, solid ground under your feet.

In your imagination, float upward a hundred feet or so and enjoy the huge increase in space you have just manifested. Infinity, filled with millions of starry rainbow points of light, is still above you, but now you are aware that it has expanded to encompass the space in front of you, behind you, and to both sides. Your perception has expanded to a whole new level. Pause for a moment to relish your new, expanded perspective. The Earth is still close by, however, comforting in its solidity.

Now float upward until the Earth dwindles below you and finally disappears from view. You immediately realize the true reality of life: The vast infinity of space, inhabited by an infinite number of stars, is actually surrounding you at all times, in all directions! You are living on a tiny spinning ball in deep space, touching infinity above, all around, and below you. Enjoy the feelings associated with floating in space—alone, surrounded by countless stars and connected to infinity above you, below you, in front of and behind you, and on both sides of you. All is one vast space, one profound silence. Take a few moments to ponder this profound insight.

There is one more step to take, however. You are still an ego floating in space, a tiny human being at the center of a vast web. Now, allow your human body to dissolve into infinity. Allow your consciousness to expand from a tiny human mind into the never-ending Universe filled with rainbow stars—tiny dots of light that are also huge, roaring, continual explosions of light that could swallow a million tiny Earths without a ripple. Allow your aware-ness to expand into the starry Universe, because this is who and what you truly are. Savor the infinity that is yourself.

This awareness of infinity creates a state of altered reality that summons inexplicable, immeasurable, and indefinable Spirit. If you are doing this meditation during the day, repeat it again on a dark, moonless, starry night.

Now, say:

Dear Spirit, I formally request that I receive your Blessing. May my spirit become strong and radiate the
Sacred out into the world.

Pause for a while and recall what has just happened. Feel it in your body.

THE DANCER

When you have fully absorbed this experience, sit down at the center of the space you have created. Focus your attention on your inner dancer. The Dancer is your divine self, the activated god or goddess that lives inside you. Dance is one of the mag-ical acts that creates the Universe, or your reality, moment by moment. The Dancer lives in the eternal present and is pure spontaneity. You have already invited Spirit to enter your awareness by consciously becoming the bridge that connects Heaven with Earth. Now, *in your imagination*, you will activate the Dancer within, your inner god or goddess who dances the dance of creation.

This ritual will help you to dance consciously, uniting the elements and Directions, in order to create the Universe according to your heart's desire. In it, you will reclaim your individuality and authenticity. You will become a unique, authentic being of light, dancing your own destiny as it unfolds.

First, state your intention:

> I now activate my inner Dancer. Come alive for me. Let
> me dance my destiny awake as I journey through
> life.

Realize that you are standing at the center of your sacred space, at the center of the Universe, uniting Heaven and Earth. Imagine the four elements surrounding you in the four Directions. Now, *in your imagination*, visualize yourself starting to move, dancing your own unique, authentic dance. Allow your body to move as it wishes, and observe yourself with love and appreciation. Enjoy your role as creator, expressing the spontaneous ecstasy of the moment. Be as creative as you wish; explore and enjoy for about thirty seconds.

Now imagine the elements rising into the air from the ground, floating and dancing around you. Direct them with your will, levitating them, spinning them, combining them, juggling them—all the time dancing your heart alive. Play! Dance with the elements for about half a minute.

Allow your body to align with the energies of the moment. Imagine your movements becoming spontaneous, unconsidered, individual, and unique to you. Imagine them as dynamic, beautiful, and full of magic.

At some point, the separate elements—Earth, Water, Air, and Fire—will start to blur and lose their individual form. They will merge and combine into the form of your dream, the new world you are dancing into existence, consciously, every instant, with every movement expressed in your dance of creation. Observe your dance of beauty and power, and acknowledge yourself as God/Goddess. Dance your own divinity for two to three minutes. When you feel complete, gently come to stillness, then say:

> I recognize and affirm that I am the Dancer at the center
> of the reality I create every instant of my life. As I
> dance, so I breathe life, meaning, and the Sacred into
> my Earthwalk.

Pause for a few seconds, then return to your physical body. Feel your skin surrounding you. When you are ready, open your eyes and physically stand up—gently, so that you don't break the energies of the moment.

Center yourself. When you are ready, become and express your Spirit Dancer *in the physical*. Start to move your body, gently at first. Start to sway, almost imperceptibly, with your eyes either open or closed. If they are open, don't allow your attention to be distracted by anything outside yourself. Let go. Lose control. Allow your body to move as it wishes.

Allow your body to move in the way *it* wants to move; don't tell it what to do. Be amazed at your body, love your body. Give your body permission to be itself and explore the space within and without expressed in the dance. Drop any judgments about how you *should* move or how dancing *should* be. Dance in a spontaneous, authentic way for about half a minute.

Don't worry if you feel uncomfortable or self-conscious. Forgive yourself for not being perfect! Express through your dance exactly how you feel. Dance through your self-consciousness! Try your best, and love yourself with all of your heart. This dance doesn't need to be beautiful; it merely needs to reflect the authentic you, in the moment. Feel everything fully—the good and the bad, the flow and the "stuckness." Dance for your joy, your healing, your wholeness. Be courageous! Be outrageous! Take risks!

As you dance, unite Above and Below and the elements through your heart. Feel the energy of the Sacred pour into your sacred circle. Imagine yourself and your space glowing and growing. Recognize yourself as the God or Goddess, creating your life at every moment, at every heartbeat, through each movement. Enjoy!

Dance your unique dance for a few minutes. When you feel complete, come gently to a stop. Sit down in the center of your circle and contemplate what has just happened for a few moments.

Become aware of your surroundings. Feel a new connection to life. Feel yourself alive, passionate, and fully empowered. See creation as a magical dance happening within you and all around you. It is the dance of life itself. Witness how the God and Goddess express their union, their ongoing act of creation, through *your* dance.

Witness how your life is an expression of the union of the God and Goddess inside you. As you dance your own dance, you channel their love. Realize how you, as your awareness increases, become more and more actively engaged in creating your life.

Imagine that your awareness becomes so bright that the God and Goddess take up permanent residence in your heart—united, creating the dance of the Universe from your core. This state is true union, the experience of One.

After a brief pause, say:

> I am the Dancer who unites Heaven and Earth. From
> now on, I manifest the Sacred into the World.

Contemplate these words for a while, then recite the Druid Prayer for Peace:

> Deep within the still center of my being, may I find
> Peace.
> Silently, within the quiet of the Grove, may I share
> Peace.
> Gently, within the greater Circle of humankind, may I
> radiate Peace.

After a few seconds, blow out the candle. Then, silently and in your own way, thank Spirit, the Earth, and the Divine Dancer for joining you in your ritual.

Write down any experiences you wish to record in your journal while they are still fresh in your mind. When you feel complete, say: "It is done. Blessed be!" Then clap your hands sharply.

Afterword and Beyond
THE CONTINUING LIFE
OF IVAN MCBETH

These closing words are not about Ivan McBeth's death. They are about his continuing, expanded life. Evidence of his living vital pulse is in the life that runs through this book. In your hands, you hold his essence in the form of his wisdom. But these are seeds harvested from his contemplative, ritualized, and dedicated life of searching within and without for love, wisdom, and power—the essence of true life, the expression of Awen.

In keeping with the ways of "Ivanism," to get where he got, you must do what he did. Read this work, and be guided and inspired by it to be engaged in this path or any other path that affirms the Spirit within you and all life. For there are gems of great wisdom in the deep mine of your mind. Dig in, dance, and dare them out. Ivan unearthed the deep pulsing power and insight of his inner spirit while finding its presence in the heart of all life. He was impeccable! And Ivan was and is *alive*. He brought this to the Druidism he loved, learned, and lived and has shared it in this sacred tome.

Who was Ivan as a man? He was son, lover, friend, guardian, consoler, jokester, dancer, poet, Druid, and a loving, loving man. He was, and eternally is, a psychopomp for the sacred landscape, a wisdom keeper, a devotee of the holy, a tickler of the soul's delight, a voice for the sacred land, a challenger of untruth, a visionary for an Earth-centered life, an erector of stone circles, a very large Lorax, and a teacher of the ancient and living Druid tradition. The wingspan of this spirit-bird was clearly far too great for its nest, and now he and his work expand. As he rises from redeemed, to blessed, to exalted Ancestor, so too will the reach of his work. So it was. So it is. So it ever shall be!

I will never forget when I first stepped with Ivan upon the holy soil of Dreamland, walked the rolling hills, mossy creeks, and stone-strewn woodland paths, and shared the longing of our hearts for the holy presence in nature. Two men loving the Earth and wanting so badly to make a difference in the restoration and preservation of our Mother, our sanctuary, our Earth. All I could think was that Fearn and Ivan were everything I ever hoped Druids could be—guardians of the woods, keepers of the stones, singers of the hearts, and bringers of healing. To me, they were living Loraxes, the spirits of the trees gifted to us by Dr. Seuss.

It was both a pleasure and a challenge to read this book and lend my heart and my hand to the writing of this afterword. One challenge was my grief—grief at the loss of Ivan's familiar shape. Another was knowing how to write a fitting coda to the continued power and wise presence of this man, my friend—a true Druid king. So, I opened my spirit as a seer and mystical writer and asked myself these four questions:

- What do we become when the last air leaves our lungs and our presence de-concentrates and expands as wide as the wind?

- Who drinks of our essence when the grapes of our being have been pressed into the wine of the soul?

The Bardic Book of Becoming

- If the gift is too big for the package, how must it be unwrapped by life and given to the lovers of its original construction?

- Where do we look for a Druid king who has spread the wings of his spirit and exploded beyond the chrysalis of his embodied shape?

Then I opened the chambers of my own heart, released the grasping childlike hands that held my mind, and followed the giggling, dancing, singing voice of a spirit who spoke in familiar tones. I heard Ivan, the Druid king, say:

Touch your heart and breathe your breath.
There is no end; there is no death.
How can this be—what do you mean?
There's a start and end to everything.
Surely these words must run in your head.
Ivan, you're silly; your heart stopped—your dead!
Quite the contrary, dear magical friend.
I share this knowing, *There is no end!*
I dance on the tips of a flitting wren's wing.
I breathe in the voice of every growing thing!
I am found in the peace of the silent stones.
I am found in the white of the stag's holy bones.
There is nowhere I cannot be found.
I am in the sea, the sky, the ground.
As you shall do, so I have done.
I spread my wings and walk on the Sun.
I swim the deeps of oceans and springs.
I pulse in the heart of all living things.
But most and more I am found in joy,

For the laughing heart is its own life buoy.
Laugh and live and dance and sing.
The joyous heart removes life's sting.
Be generous, be kind; be loving and true.
And beyond form, I—and the magic—
Will be waiting for you.
Love is eternal!

Orion Foxwood, author of *The Flame in the Cauldron*

ABOUT THE AUTHORS

 **Ivan McBeth**, a Druid in the Order of Bards, Ovates, and Druids (OBOD), founded the Green Mountain Druid Order, a modern mystery school based in Worcester, Vermont together with his partner Fearn Lickfield. Ivan's passion was the creation of sacred space, especially stone circles. A founding member of the Circles for Peace project in the United States, he was co-responsible for the Burlington Earth Clock and over twenty-five other full-sized stone circles around the world, including the large Swan Circle on the site of the Glastonbury Music Festival in the UK and the Kinstone Megalithic Garden in Wisconsin. Ivan died in 2016.

 **Fearn Lickfield** is web weaver and facilitator of the re-connection of the hearts of people with the Heart of Nature. She is director of The Green Mountain Druid School and teaches Guardians of the Sacred Earth. She works as a certified flower-essence practitioner, geomancer, dowser, ecstatic-dance leader, community organizer, gardener, and medicine maker. Being a lover of magic and ritual, she creates and leads community celebrations in honor of the earth and waters, the seasons, and for rites of passage. Fearn is steward of Dreamland, a sanctuary and mystery school in Worcester, VT. Visit her at *www.greenmountaindruidorder.org*

TO OUR READERS

Weiser Books, an imprint of Red Wheel / Weiser, publishes books across the entire spectrum of occult, esoteric, speculative, and New Age subjects. Our mission is to publish quality books that will make a difference in people's lives without advocating any one particular path or field of study. We value the integrity, originality, and depth of knowledge of our authors.

Our readers are our most important resource, and we appreciate your input, suggestions, and ideas about what you would like to see published.

Visit our website at *www.redwheelweiser.com* to learn about our upcoming books and free downloads, and be sure to go to *www.redwheelweiser.com / newsletter* to sign up for newsletters and exclusive offers.

You can also contact us at *info@rwwbooks.com* or at

Red Wheel / Weiser, LLC
65 Parker Street, Suite 7
Newburyport, MA 01950